Bringing Micro to the Macro

The field of human services is filled with clinicians turned managers. Many of these managers have not studied business and lack leadership and management experience. *Bringing Micro to the Macro: Adapting Clinical Interventions for Supervision and Management* shows social workers and other human service professionals how to adapt their clinical and direct practice skills to be effective supervisors and managers.

The book demonstrates the parallels between the micro process of client work and the macro process of staff supervision and management. It also shows managers how to properly adapt and employ their micro practice skills to engage, motivate, and guide their staff to achieve maximum impact and productivity. The first four parts are based on the four phases of service delivery in social work: Engagement, Assessment, Intervention, and Evaluation and Termination. The book concludes with a part on Self-Care, as this is important if you want to have longevity in this field.

Bringing Micro to the Macro is a user-friendly book that can be a tool that new supervisors or managers in social work and human services can reach for when they wonder how to work with staff instead of clients.

Ruth Supranovich is Clinical Associate Professor and Director of Field Education at the Suzanne Dworak-Peck School of Social Work at the University of Southern California. She has extensive experience as a case manager, clinician, supervisor, manager, and leader in government and non-profit social service agencies.

Richard Newmyer is Senior Lecturer with the Suzanne Dworak-Peck School of Social Work at the University of Southern California. He spent two decades developing programs for children, youth, and families. His experience includes administration, facilitation, community organizing, governmental relations, social advocacy, communications, and fundraising.

Supranovich and Newmyer have written an excellent, easy-to-read guide for human services professionals making the transition from direct practice into supervision and management. Many professionals with advanced degrees may be quickly promoted to supervisory positions in response to personal or organizational changes. This book builds upon and leverages the value of that clinical training to new administrative roles, responsibilities and effective leadership.

Marleen Wong, *Senior Vice Dean, David Lawrence Stein/Violet Goldberg Sachs Professor of Mental Health and Fellow of the American Academy of Social Work and Social Welfare*

As a Director of a community-based youth serving non-profit organization, I have been looking for a book like this to support succession planning for my staff. For those of us in the human services field who began working in the 1980s, management and leadership training primarily emerged from the school of hard knocks and trying to extrapolate from our human service training on how to manage people, organizations, and missions. It is exciting to see trusted social work practitioners and educators expanding this experience into a recognizable model to develop our future human services leaders.

Don Stump, *Executive Director, North County Lifeline*

A beautifully constructed juxtaposition of supervision and clinical practice. Supranovich and Newmyer offer insightful personal narratives along with a careful review of the literature that will both inform and move the audience into improved managerial practices for beginning and experienced leaders alike. A human-centered approach that incorporates best practices within a novel framework. *Bringing Micro to the Macro* will be sure to transform how we think about supervision and serve as a hands-on guide in the preparation and support of health and human service practitioners.

Eugenia L. Weiss, *Co-author*, Leadership with Impact: Preparing Health and Human Service Practitioners in the age of Innovation and Diversity

Bringing Micro to the Macro

Adapting Clinical Interventions for Supervision and Management

Ruth Supranovich and
Richard Newmyer

NEW YORK AND LONDON

First published 2021
by Routledge
52 Vanderbilt Avenue, New York, NY 10017

and by Routledge
2 Park Square, Milton Park, Abingdon, Oxon, OX14 4RN

Routledge is an imprint of the Taylor & Francis Group, an informa business

© 2021 Taylor & Francis

The right of Ruth Supranovich and Richard Newmyer to be identified as authors of this work has been asserted by them in accordance with sections 77 and 78 of the Copyright, Designs and Patents Act 1988.

All rights reserved. No part of this book may be reprinted or reproduced or utilised in any form or by any electronic, mechanical, or other means, now known or hereafter invented, including photocopying and recording, or in any information storage or retrieval system, without permission in writing from the publishers.

Trademark notice: Product or corporate names may be trademarks or registered trademarks, and are used only for identification and explanation without intent to infringe.

Library of Congress Cataloging-in-Publication Data
Names: Supranovich, Ruth, author. | Newmyer, Richard, author.
Title: Bringing micro to the macro : adapting clinical interventions for
    supervision and management / Ruth Supranovich and Richard
    Newmyer.
Description: New York, NY : Routledge Books, 2020. | Includes
    bibliographical references and index.
Identifiers: LCCN 2020010542 (print) | LCCN 2020010543 (ebook) |
    ISBN 9781138349551 (hardback) | ISBN 9781138349605 (paperback) |
    ISBN 9780429436277 (ebook)
Subjects: LCSH: Social work administration. | Social workers—Supervision of. |
    Social case work—Management.
Classification: LCC HV41 .S8696 2020 (print) | LCC HV41 (ebook) |
    DDC 361.3068—dc23
LC record available at https://lccn.loc.gov/2020010542
LC ebook record available at https://lccn.loc.gov/2020010543

ISBN: 978-1-138-34955-1 (hbk)
ISBN: 978-1-138-34960-5 (pbk)
ISBN: 978-0-429-43627-7 (ebk)

Typeset in Bembo
by Apex CoVantage, LLC

Printed in the United Kingdom
by Henry Ling Limited

Contents

Acknowledgments		vii
Introduction		1
PART ONE		
Engagement		3
1	Establishing a Working Alliance	5
2	Setting Expectations	13
3	Orienting and Onboarding	20
PART TWO		
Assessment		29
4	Observation	31
5	Interviewing	37
6	Assessment Tools	44
PART THREE		
Intervention		53
7	Crisis Management	55
8	Resistance to Change	63
9	Performance Issues	71

vi *Contents*

PART FOUR
Evaluation & Termination 81

10 Staff Development 83

11 Periodic Review and Performance Monitoring 92

12 Termination 101

PART FIVE
Self-Care 109

13 Boundaries 111

14 Vicarious Trauma and Secondary Traumatic Stress 120

15 Work-Life Balance 129

Index 136

Acknowledgments

We want to thank our colleagues for providing feedback, encouragement, and inspiration, with special thanks to Juan Carlos Araque, Pam Franzwa, Laura Gale, Omar Lopez, Tom Packard, Eugenia Weiss, and Leslie Wind. Thanks to Aaron Cohen for his excellent copyediting skills. This book would not have been possible without the love and support of our wonderful families and friends, in particular our spouses/partners, Sayandro and Jessica.

Introduction

This book is the culmination of many years of conversations between the authors. We both graduated with our Master of Social Work degrees (MSWs) from the same university, one with a clinical focus (Ruth) and the other on the administrative track (Rick). Since graduating over 25 years ago, our paths have crossed professionally many times, most recently as professors at the University of Southern California (USC). The USC Suzanne Dworak-Peck School of Social Work has an emphasis on the science of social work and we have both participated in training students in various evidence based practices (EBPs). It was during these trainings that we began to talk about how the EBPs we were teaching were very similar to the skills we had both used as supervisors, managers, and leaders in social services prior to joining academia. We began referring to this as "Taking Micro to the Macro."

We wanted to write a user-friendly book that could be a tool that new supervisors or managers in social work and human services could reach for when they wondered, like we had when we started out, what they are supposed to do now that they have staff instead of clients. We assume a baseline of basic social work skills that are common across many disciplines, but also include a brief refresher on each of the practice skills being discussed as a point of reference for the subsequent application to macro practice.

We have organized the book into five parts. The first four parts are based on four phases of service delivery in social work: Engagement, Assessment, Intervention, and Evaluation & Termination. We end the book with a part on Self-Care, as this is important if you want to have longevity in this field. Each chapter begins with a true story from our work experience that illustrates the topic to be discussed. After a brief introduction we have called the "overture" (like the orchestral teaser at the beginning of a musical), we then describe the practice area first as it looks in the micro arena and then how it looks in the macro arena. Our intention is to show the reader how their practice as a supervisor or manager is very similar to that of a direct service provider, with some minor adaptations. To make this book accessible and easy to use in your day-to-day work, each chapter has a table called "This Is How We Do It" and a section of "Key Takeaways." This can serve as a quick reference and summary of the prior macro section.

This book cannot hope to cover everything you will encounter in your role as a supervisor or manager, but it will hopefully reassure you that you already have all the skills you need to be successful.

Part One

Engagement

Engagement is the first stage of treatment and a critical step when starting in a new position as a supervisor or manager and beginning to work with a new staff person or workgroup. The following three chapters will discuss how building a strong therapeutic alliance is similar to building a strong supervisory working alliance (Chapter 1); explore how the tools and processes used to set expectations for clinical work have their equivalents in the supervisory context (Chapter 2); and consider how orienting an employee to the workplace is similar to how a clinician prepares a client to receive services (Chapter 3). These three areas of practice come together to establish the rules of engagement and create a trusting partnership between supervisor and supervisee.

1 Establishing a Working Alliance

Once Upon a Time

At the tender age of 25, I was hired as a home visitor by a child abuse prevention agency. The job entailed going into the homes of complete strangers and teaching them parenting skills. I was uniquely qualified for the job with my bachelor's degree in psychology, VW camper van, and utter lack of experience. On the plus side, I had no children of my own, am the youngest in my family, and had never even worked as a babysitter. After securing the job, I had to ask, "Why did you hire me?" My new boss replied, "Because, if you knocked on the door of my house, I would let you in. The rest we can teach you." She went on to explain that I came across as warm, interested, and friendly. I was likeable, and that was something she could not teach. I heard a very similar remark when I was hired for my first management job ten years later. The director who hired me said, "I think the staff are going to like you and I can send you to management training to learn the other stuff." When it was my turn to hire supervisors and managers for my organization, I never underestimated the importance of likeability.

While human services work is not a popularity contest, the reality is that your staff will be more inclined to talk with you and work on goals if they like you and believe you like them. The relationship you establish in your first meeting together provides the foundation for everything to come after.

Overture

Whether providing direct services to clients or supervision or management as an administrator, the term "social work" says it all! Our work is social – we use our social skills to connect with others to get things done. There is no manual, as you would have for a machine, with directions on how to use it, that works every time. The lack of predictability in human services requires social flexibility, and you really have to enjoy people to embrace this world of work. Whether it be an individual or a group, our work is to engage socially and build relationships, improve the social experiences of

6　*Engagement*

others, and ultimately to improve society. Whether doing clinical work or management, it is all about relationships. The talents, skills, and experience you have developed in relationship building as a direct service provider are what will make you a great supervisor and manager – with a few adaptations. This first challenge of building a strong working alliance with your employees is a great place to examine the transferability of your direct practice skill set.

The Micro Arena

The helping professional's relationship with his or her client, often referred to as the "therapeutic alliance" in the psychotherapy and counseling literature, is generally regarded as a crucial factor in the success of the encounter (Meissner, 1996; Safran, 2010). The therapeutic alliance is one of the most widely researched variables, with several meta-analyses showing clear linkages between the quality of the therapeutic alliance and treatment outcomes (Safran, 2010). Research has also shown that a strong therapeutic alliance can mediate suicidal behaviors, demonstrating just how critical it is to clinical outcomes (Dunster-Page, Berry, Wainwright, & Haddock, 2017). An effective therapeutic alliance can literally save lives.

The literature has described factors that can enhance this alliance, such as empathic attunement (Meissner, 1996); rapport, trust, and caring (Shulman, 2012); as well as agreement to work on tasks together and a process of negotiation (Safran, 2010). Two groups of researchers working in the area of children's mental health studied which engagement methods were most effective in creating a working alliance with children and families (e.g., assessment, accessibility, and psychoeducation) and how and when to employ them (Becker et al., 2013; Lindsay, Proulx, Scott, & Thomson, 2013). Engagement and establishing the trust needed to build a strong and effective therapeutic alliance is the foundation of good social work practice.

The Macro Arena

Correlates between the therapeutic and the supervisory alliance can be found throughout the literature on supervision of counselors and psychotherapists. This crossover was initially a psychoanalytic framework (Bordin, 1983), with subsequent research confirming that a strong emotional bond between the supervisor and supervisee positively impacted employee satisfaction (Ladany, Ellis, & Friedlander, 1999) and helped to moderate workplace stressors and prevent burnout (Sterner, 2009). The qualities of a positive supervisory working alliance include familiar concepts to those providing direct services on a daily basis: non-judgment, empathy, validation, exploration, and normalization of anxiety and tension (Sterner, 2009). The behaviors listed as obstacles to building this supervisory working alliance will again be familiar to those working with clients: being critical, disrespectful, unsupportive, inattentive, and lacking trust, openness, praise, and encouragement (Sterner, 2009).

As in the early stages of the therapeutic relationship, the supervisory relationship helps address motivation. In this case, examples include exploring the employee's level of motivation, the possible causes for low motivation, and instilling hope and inspiration for a better future. Knowing their supervisor is interested in discussing their concerns – regardless of whether an immediate solution emerges – will help solidify the working alliance, which will bode well for future meetings and likely result in a boost in enthusiasm until further discussions can occur. As with therapy, the goal is not only for the employee to come back for another appointment, but also to begin to contemplate the benefits of engaging in a relationship with their assigned supervisor. Later in this book, we will go into more detail about the use of Motivational Interviewing (MI) techniques in supervision and management, but the basic communication skills of asking open-ended questions, using affirmations, reflection, and summarization (OARS), are an essential part of the supervisor-supervisee meeting just as they are with the clinician-client encounter.

Motivation has been addressed extensively in the management literature and is identified as the most frequent cause of performance problems (Clark & Estes, 2008). With over 80% of workers admitting they could work harder at their job and almost 50% stating they do the bare minimum to keep their jobs (Spitzer, 1995), creating a strong working alliance that enhances an employee's motivation to engage in his or her work can have a significant impact on the organization and ultimately better serve customers, clients, or patients. Most of us working in the helping professions do so because we want to make a difference in the lives of those struggling with addiction, abuse, poverty, mental illness, and any other number of social ills. As a supervisor or manager, if you can effectively engage and motivate your employees to perform even 20% better, consider how you can potentially make a positive difference in the lives of so many more people through them.

Leader-Member Exchange (LMX) is an example of a management theory that focuses on the dyadic relationship between a manager and a worker (Northouse, 2013). There are two main types of relationships: in-group and out-group. In-group relationships (i.e., high-quality LMX) are characterized by healthy communication, trust, and mutual respect; in contrast, out-group relationships (i.e., low-quality LMX) are characterized by formal communication, lack of trust, and individual self-interest. An in-group dyad is a true relationship, while an out-group dyad is more of a transaction. In-group dyads have been linked to a range of positive outcomes, including improved performance, job satisfaction, and retention (Breevaart, Bakker, Demerouti, & van den Heuvel, 2015; Hopkins, 2002; Masterson, Lewis, Goldman, & Taylor, 2000; Wayne, Shore, & Liden, 1997).

Perceived Organizational Support (POS) refers to the employee's perception of the extent to which the organization values his or her contribution and

8   *Engagement*

cares about him or her as a person (Eisenberger, Huntington, Hutchison, & Sowa, 1986). When employees believe they are valued and cared for, they usually reciprocate it. POS is correlated with improved job performance, greater worker satisfaction, and reduced turnover intention (Kurtessis et al., 2015). Establishing a high-quality LMX dyad with each direct report will help you build the foundation for high POS. As a result, your staff will feel appreciated, valued, and respected – bringing their "A" game to the organization and the clients and community you serve.

Same but Different

Despite the similarities between the therapeutic working alliance and the supervisory working alliance, it is important to know the limits of your new role; you are the supervisor and not the therapist. Even when looking at the parallels between counseling and supervising, you do not treat each staff meeting as a therapy session. At the same time, you should not turn into an emotionally inaccessible, authoritarian boss. Working in the gray areas and managing relationships is another skill set you already possess. As a clinician or case manager, you know how to set boundaries, define your role, and adhere to ethical guidelines related to conflicts of interest. As with direct practice, you may need to seek guidance and regular consultation to navigate the relationship and the inevitable ethical dilemmas that will arise.

For example, it can be challenging to supervise someone you suspect is suffering from depression. You may be one of the best Cognitive Behavioral Therapy (CBT) clinicians around and know some of the best psychiatrists when it comes to treating depression, but you are not your employee's therapist. Does this mean you cannot acknowledge their symptoms and share helpful resources? If you ignore the obvious signs, how will they feel cared about and how might that impact your working alliance? These are good questions, often resulting in the supervisor taking one of two extremes: either becoming the staff therapist or reacting in the opposite direction and initiating severe discipline processes. As a supervisor, you will need to engage your tolerance for ambiguity and abstruseness, just as you did as a direct service practitioner.

This Is How We Do It

The thread that ties everything together is the importance of relationship building and communication between you and your staff. As a new manager (or even as an experienced manager), your primary vehicle for doing so is spending time with your direct reports. The process is not complicated – the key is doing it intentionally and consistently. The following table includes key aspects of your role as supervisor, as well as the "what" and "why" behind each action.

Establishing a Working Alliance 9

Table 1.1

Component	What to Do	Purpose
Schedule individual time	• Meet regularly with each of your direct reports • Avoid canceling or rescheduling • Eliminate or minimize interruptions • Provide a safe space for honest conversations	• Making time for the people who are important to us • Having regular meetings ensures we go beyond status reports and putting out fires
Ask good questions	• Be curious • Listen genuinely • Ask follow-up questions • Pay attention to non-verbal communication	• When we care about people, we want to know more about them • We learn more by asking questions than giving directives
Keep notes	• Build on past discussions • Show you are listening and care about what they have to say	• Do not risk forgetting what was discussed • We strengthen rapport by building on past discussions

Case Study

When José, a supervisor of case managers, met with a new employee, Shari, he enquired about her prior work experience. Shari told him that in her prior job she felt undervalued because she was never given challenging assignments and felt micro-managed. José noticed Shari became agitated when describing her prior manager. José was vaguely familiar with Shari's prior supervisor and had a positive impression of this individual, so he became curious about Shari's experience. José had been a clinician prior to his promotion to supervisor and he found himself wondering about Shari's childhood and whether her parents were overly protective, whether she successfully resolved the autonomy versus shame and doubt phase of child development, and how he might be able to provide her with a more corrective experience. He wanted to ask about Shari's childhood and explore her internal conflicts (psychoanalytic) or begin to dig down to explore her core beliefs (cognitive-behavioral). Instead, remembering that he was now the supervisor, José switched to the important work of employee engagement and creating a positive supervisory bond. José empathized with Shari's prior experience [*empathy*] and thanked her for candidly

10   *Engagement*

sharing her concerns [*affirmation*]. He suggested they talk about this going forward so that he was sufficiently supportive of Shari's professional growth [*shared tasks and openness to negotiation*]. José asked Shari to describe what "micro-managing" looked like in her prior position and what type of management style she preferred [*open-ended questions, clarification, interest, and caring*]. He reflected what he heard to reach a shared understanding [*reflection*]. José told Shari that he may be a little overinvolved initially as Shari learned more about her new position, the workplace, and her new responsibilities, but he invited Shari to tell him if she felt that he was being overly intrusive, especially over time [*psychoeducation and openness to negotiation*]. José made a note in his file to check in on this during future meetings.

Terrell was another case manager and when he arrived for supervision with José, he looked pale and sad. Terrell said he was experiencing a rough time in his life, was having difficulty sleeping, and as a result was struggling to stay focused at work. José observed that Terrell had dark rings under his eyes, was slouched in his chair, and spoke in a monotone voice. He wanted to ask about Terrell's physical and mental health, family situation, personal stressors, as well as whether he had sought help for his personal and sleep issues or considered an assessment for possible depression. José thought about his role and focused on being caring and employee-focused without trying to become Terrell's therapist. To do this, José did not abandon his empathic responses and stated, "Your sleeping difficulties are really affecting your life and this seems distressing to you" [*reflection/empathic response*]. Then, rather than adding "tell me more," José was more specific and stated, "Tell me more about how this is affecting you at work" [*open-ended question/assessment*]. José kept the conversation focused on the workplace while still encouraging Terrell to talk. As a result, Terrell shared that because he was not sleeping well at night, by mid-afternoon he lost focus. With his head down, he described feeling embarrassed to admit he had fallen asleep during a recent multi-disciplinary case consultation. Terrell was worried this would affect his reputation and, even more, that he may fall asleep during a meeting with a client. José learned that Terrell was a very dedicated employee and was concerned about his performance. Despite his clinical curiosity, he did not ask why Terrell thought he was having difficulty sleeping or if anything recently had triggered his sleeping issues. Instead, José stated, "I can tell you are really worried about how this is affecting your work and I appreciate you letting me know. Do you have a plan as to how to get some relief and get back on track?" [*agreement on goals and tasks*]. Terrell stated he had an appointment scheduled with his doctor and José praised him for taking this step [*affirmation*]. He also provided him with a leaflet about the Employee Assistance Program as a possible resource. José asked if there was anything he could do to support him at work, to which Terrell said,

"I just appreciate you listening and being understanding and I assure you I will get this resolved. I was thinking I could try and see more clients in the mornings rather than the afternoon for the time being if that's OK." José agreed that this was a good idea [*agreement on goals and tasks*]. He then thanked Terrell for sharing this situation as well as his proactive stance in getting help for himself while also attending to his clients [*summarization and affirmation*].

In both cases, José listened, validated, and praised the employees, demonstrating non-judgment and respect as well as openness and transparency. Moreover, José acknowledged the problem and recognized the employee's motivation to actively work on a solution. Using clinical skills within the bounds of his role as a supervisor, he built a strong alliance between supervisor and employee, organization and employee, and, ultimately, between employee and client.

Key Takeaways

- It is all about the relationship between you and your worker.
- A good relationship includes healthy communication, trust, and mutual respect.
- High-quality relationships with your direct reports will reap benefits for your organization and the people you serve.

Discussion Questions

1. What can you do to build positive rapport with your new hires?
2. What steps can you take to build trust with your direct reports?
3. In cases where you have less than positive rapport with your direct reports, what can you do to move your working relationship in a more positive, productive direction?

References

Becker, K. D., Lee, B. R., Daleiden, E. L., Lindsey, M., Brandt, N. E., & Chorpita, B. F. (2013). The common elements of engagement in children's mental health services: Which elements for which outcomes? *Journal of Clinical Child & Adolescent Psychology, 44*(1), 30–43. https://doi.org/10.1080/15374416.2013.814543

Bordin, E. S. (1983). A working alliance based model of supervision. *The Counseling Psychologist, 11*(1), 35–42. https://doi.org/10.1177/0011000083111007

Breevaart, K., Bakker, A. B., Demerouti, E., & van den Heuvel, M. (2015). Leader-member exchange, work engagement, and job performance. *Journal of Managerial Psychology, 30*(7), 754–770. https://doi.org/10.1108/jmp-03-2013-0088

Clark, R. E., & Estes, F. (2008). *Turning research into results: A guide to selecting the right performance solutions.* Charlotte, NC: Information Age Publishing, Inc.

Dunster-Page, C. A., Berry, K., Wainwright, L., & Haddock, G. (2017). An exploratory study into therapeutic alliance, defeat, entrapment and suicidality on mental health wards. *Journal of Psychiatric and Mental Health Nursing, 25*(2), 119–130. https://doi.org/10.1111/jpm.12444

Eisenberger, R., Huntington, R., Hutchison, S., & Sowa, D. (1986). *Survey of Perceived Organizational Support (SPOS)* [Database record]. APA PsycTests. https://doi.org/10.1037/t01207-000

Hopkins, K. M. (2002). Organizational citizenship in social service agencies. *Administration in Social Work, 26*(2), 1–15. https://doi.org/10.1300/J147v26n02_01

Kurtessis, J. N., Eisenberger, R., Ford, M. T., Buffardi, L. C., Stewart, K. A., & Adis, C. S. (2015). Perceived organizational support: A meta-analytic evaluation of organizational support theory. *Journal of Management, 43*(6), 1854–1884. https://doi.org/10.1177/0149206315575554

Ladany, N., Ellis, M. V., & Friedlander, M. L. (1999). The supervisory working alliance, trainee self-efficacy, and satisfaction. *Journal of Counseling & Development, 77*(4), 447–455. https://doi.org/fx87ht

Lindsay, S., Proulx, M., Scott, H., & Thomson, N. (2013). Exploring teachers' strategies for including children with autism spectrum disorder in mainstream classrooms. *International Journal of Inclusive Education, 18*(2), 101–122. https://doi.org/10.1080/13603116.2012.758320

Masterson, S. S., Lewis, K., Goldman, B. M., & Taylor, M. S. (2000). Integrating justice and social exchange: The differing effects of fair procedures and treatment on work relationships. *Academy of Management Journal, 43*(4), 738–748. https://doi.org/10.2307/1556364

Meissner, W. (1996). Empathy in the therapeutic alliance. *Psychoanalytic Inquiry, 16*(1), 39–53. https://doi.org/10.1080/07351699609534063

Northouse, P. G. (2013). *Leadership: Theory and practice* (6th ed.). Los Angeles, CA: SAGE.

Safran, J. D. (2010). Therapeutic alliance. *The Corsini Encyclopedia of Psychology.* https://doi.org/10.1002/9780470479216.corpsy0992

Shulman, L. (2012). *The skills of helping individuals, families, groups, and communities* (7th ed.). Belmont, CA: Cengage Learning.

Spitzer, D. (1995). *SuperMotivation: A blueprint for energizing your organization from top to bottom.* New York: AMACOM Books.

Sterner, W. (2009). Influence of the supervisory working alliance on supervisee work satisfaction and work-related stress. *Journal of Mental Health Counseling, 31*(3), 249–263. https://doi.org/dj6j

Wayne, S. J., Shore, L. M., & Liden, R. C. (1997). Perceived organizational support and leader- member exchange: A social exchange perspective. *Academy of Management Journal, 40*(1), 82–111. https://doi.org/10.2307/257021

2 Setting Expectations

Once Upon a Time

I must be honest: I panicked a little when I was offered my first management position at a child abuse prevention agency. I had trained as a clinician and my only supervisory experience was as a field instructor for student interns. I did not know where to begin and did not want to admit my trepidation to the person who hired me. So, I reached out to a friend who had taken a more traditional administrative path to ask for her advice. She handed me a copy of "First, Break All the Rules" by Marcus Buckingham and Curt Coffman and said, "Start with the first three questions." If you have not read this book, I highly recommend you do so (immediately after you finish reading this one, of course). At the very least, review the 12 questions the authors provide as essential ingredients in building an engaged workforce.

Question one asks, "Do I know what is expected of me at work?" (Buckingham & Coffman, 1999, p. 33). I decided this would be the focus of my first week as a program manager. First, I scheduled one-on-one meetings with my direct reports. In preparation, I reviewed their job descriptions and personnel files. When I met with each of my staff – after some general "get-acquainted" conversation – I said that one of the most important things at work is knowing what is expected of us. I then asked each person what they expected from me as a supervisor. Their immediate responses ranged from wide eyes to blank stares. Eventually, one case manager said, "I don't think anyone's ever asked me that before." Another said, "I don't know, what do *you* expect from *me*?" And yet another gave me a long list of things she wanted, many of which were clearly unmet by her prior boss, and others which were quite unrealistic. I could not complain – I literally asked for it.

Despite the awkwardness, it turned out to be an excellent first question. We explored everything from the nuts and bolts of each other's roles and communication styles to accessibility. I have asked this same question of every person I have supervised since. After all, how will I know what is expected of me if I do not ask the very people I am there to serve and support? Additionally, asking your direct reports what they expect from you can help prevent some major misunderstandings by clarifying, and perhaps challenging, expectations (Direct Report #3: No, I can't take you out for lunch each week!).

14   *Engagement*

Overture

We all like to know what we are getting into, as evidenced by the popularity of Yelp, Rotten Tomatoes, Tinder, and many other websites that guide us on what to expect from our restaurants, movies, and blind dates. Likewise, when we are looking for a job, we do our research, ask colleagues what they know about the organization, and carefully read the job description to see if it seems like a good fit. Whether as a client seeking social services or a human services professional seeking a job, clear and realistic expectations are critical for a successful experience.

The Micro Arena

The role of expectations in client services has been studied extensively. Constantino, Ametrano, and Greenberg (2012) conducted a review of the research on the role of expectations in psychotherapy, finding that assessing, addressing (through education and socialization), negotiating, and monitoring treatment expectations as well as clarifying expected length of treatment were key to successful treatment outcomes for clients. Even before initiating services, potential clients need to know what to expect. For example, Elliott, Westmacott, Hunsley, Rumstein-McKean, and Best (2015) found that the most distressing aspect of help-seeking was the realization that problems were related to mental health and that therapy could help. Messaging on websites and in waiting rooms helped to clarify expectations in this regard by providing information about mental health symptoms and the potential of therapy to ameliorate these symptoms. The next challenge the authors identified was to get clients to come in for services and come back. This time, the critical factor was providing education and information about the value of a strong therapeutic alliance, guiding the client with respect to their and the therapist's responsibilities, and explaining what the client could realistically expect to gain from the relationship.

Understanding the client's expectations is also important. Based on a study of depressed adolescent psychotherapy clients, Weitkamp, Klein, Hofmann, Wiegand-Grefe, and Midgley (2017) found that fostering realistic treatment and outcome expectations required paying careful attention to the specific expectations of the young person. Likewise, Hepworth, Rooney, Rooney, and Strom-Gottfried (2017) pointed out that client expectations are often very different from those of social workers, especially for mandated clients. The authors suggested that when working with involuntary clients, understanding the client's expectations should be the top priority.

As a service provider, you probably do a number of things to educate new clients and prepare them for what to expect from the experience. You, or your organization, have thought carefully about how to introduce your services to clients and provide a structure for service delivery with identified client inputs and agency outputs. Well-designed forms such as informed consent or service agreements include many aspects of the contractual relationship between service provider and client, such as the risks and benefits of treatment, record keeping, confidentiality limits, client-therapist privilege, fee arrangements, and cancellation and termination policies. Likely, these aspects are reviewed in detail before the working relationship begins and revisited when issues arise. Knowing who does what and the rules of engagement guiding the agency-client interaction not only sets the client up for success, but also assures more efficient and cost-effective service delivery. Reflecting on this and identifying best practices in direct service delivery will set you up well as a supervisor or manager, particularly when it comes to setting expectations for your direct reports.

The Macro Arena

"First, Break All the Rules," referenced in this chapter's opening story, is based on data gathered by the Gallup Organization from in-depth interviews with over 80,000 managers in over 400 companies (Buckingham & Coffman, 1999). Though most managers interviewed were from private industry and for-profit organizations, the 12 questions that emerged from this research apply just as well to management practice in health and human services. The 12 questions resonate in a human services environment by identifying a hierarchy to the questions akin to Maslow's (1943) "hierarchy of needs." Employees must have their basic needs met first before they can benefit from higher-order supervisory experiences. In supervision and management, the basics are described in question one, "Do I know what is expected of me at work?" (Buckingham & Coffman, 1999, p. 28).

The Gallup Organization is not the only research group to identify clear expectations as the cornerstone of effective supervision and management. Many texts aimed at new supervisors and managers highlight the importance of clarifying expectations as a first step, and, sadly, noting the frequency with which this step is overlooked (Neff & Citrin, 2007; Woodbury, Cohen, & Zayszly, 2001). Establishing clear expectations with your direct reports is essential to fostering engagement and preventing misunderstandings and confusion (Miehls, Everett, Segal, & du Bois, 2013).

As you may have gathered, the premise of this book is that you can take your clinical prowess and apply it effectively in your new role as the supervisor or manager. As a direct practitioner, you may have used consent for treatment forms in outpatient care, "house rules" at a residential facility, or a service contract at a social service agency. There are equivalent processes in place to set the stage for the employer-employee relationship. If you work for a larger agency that has a human resources (HR) department, your direct report likely signed a variety of forms related to the organizational rules and policies during the hiring process. As a clinician or social worker, one of your first tasks before beginning service delivery is to make sure your client has reviewed, understood, and signed any organizational paperwork, and this same best practice applies as a supervisor. You will want to examine your supervisee's file to note which forms they have signed and review their job description, any prior performance appraisals, and current performance goals. You will then want to make sure from the first meeting that the employee knows what you know and that you develop a shared understanding of the agency policies, procedures, and expectations.

16 *Engagement*

During that first clinical session or client meeting, you will inevitably need to address policies about missed appointments and their consequences. Likewise, you will need to discuss basics such as timekeeping and schedules with your staff. Even in the largest bureaucracies with the most elaborate policies and procedures manuals, what is written in black and white is rarely quite so clear-cut in practice. The employee manual may say that staff must arrive and leave work at a designated time and take specific breaks throughout the day, but rarely is work life that simple in a social service agency working with complex clients with complex needs. When taking over supervision of an existing team, it is especially important that you discuss how they currently manage their time (they will be operating under the prior supervisor's expectations) and provide a rationale if you plan to change this expectation. It is also essential to discuss the consequences of failing to live up to those expectations, which will be dictated not only by agency rules but also by how you as a supervisor or manager apply them. Of course, *you* will need to be very clear about what is expected of *you* in this regard also. For example, you do not want to tell your staff that you expect them to eat at their desks and work through lunch unpaid (even if you personally employ this unhealthy work behavior), opening your agency up to labor law violations.

Another way to establish expectations as a direct service provider is to create a case plan or set treatment goals. Sometimes these goals will come from the clients, but they can also include requirements dictated by a court, school, or parent. This goal-setting activity usually articulates not only what the outcome will be for the client, but also what the two of you will be doing toward that end. While we will discuss goal setting and case planning in more detail in Chapter 10, it is important to note at this juncture that this activity is a critical aspect of establishing expectations as a supervisor or manager. When first meeting with new employees, there is invariably some other entity that has set some goals (e.g., investigate allegations of elder abuse, help veterans find housing, or educate parents on positive parenting skills). Your agency might have a specific intervention or approach that the new employee needs to be made aware of, trained to provide, and agrees to as a valid treatment model. As the supervisor, you can engage in a similar process of goal setting as you would in direct practice but with the added benefit that employees have usually elected to work at the agency and likely already share the program mission and goals. While this is not always the case – even the most engaged employees may balk at changes in how they practice if the agency adopts a new intervention – the fact that the employee gets paid to work with you may make this task a little easier at first. (Not to worry; resistance to change is something you will surely encounter as a supervisor or manager and we will cover this further in Chapter 8).

This Is How We Do It

If you have done clinical work, we believe you will find that the process of setting expectations with your staff is quite similar to doing so with your clients. In both cases, it is important to have things in writing and ensure there is informed consent from the beginning as well as throughout the process. The following table synthesizes key micro and macro actions and their inter-relationship.

Setting Expectations 17

Table 2.1

Micro/Client	*Macro/Direct Report*
Complete forms (e.g., consent to treat, residential "house rules," service contract, etc.)	Complete forms (e.g., acknowledgment of policies, emergency contacts, equipment use, or employment contract)
Review forms to be sure client understands what they are signing	Review forms to be sure employee understands what they are signing
Review referral and existing case file if applicable, speak with referring party if other than the client	Review personnel file, job description, prior performance appraisals if available
Review expectations for treatment (e.g., communication, payment, attendance, length of treatment, etc.)	Review agency policies, procedures, and expectations (e.g., timekeeping, leave requests, and reimbursements)
Create a case plan and/or set treatment goals with the client and include goals set by external entities if relevant (e.g., courts or school)	Identify professional development goals and/or communicate agency goals and employee's role in meeting them
Provide psychoeducation as to treatment approaches you will use and describe clinician and client responsibilities (e.g., describe what CBT is and that client may have some "homework")	Establish if supervisee is familiar with services provided and if not provide training on commonly used interventions (e.g., MI, CBT, seeking safety, etc.)
Identify behavioral indicators that will let you and the client know that treatment is working (e.g., decreased feelings of depression, increased positive interactions with parents, etc.)	Identify behavioral indicators that will let you and the supervisee know that they are performing as expected (e.g., number of clients seen weekly, timely submission of documentation, etc.)
Instill hope and praise small accomplishments	Instill hope and praise small accomplishments

Case Study

Pam was a new case manager at an employment development agency. On her first day, she met briefly with her supervisor, who gave her a list of clients to call and set up monthly appointments to work on helping them get a job. Pam eagerly called her new clients and set up meetings.

Judy was also new to the agency but reported to a different supervisor in a different office. In addition to giving her a list of client names, her supervisor told her about the agency mission and goals. The supervisor also let Judy know that the agency had a contract with the state government and that the contract required them to complete a number of tasks with their clients. These included the following: 100% of clients must create a resume within one month, submit three job applications every month, and be employed at least part-time within 12 months. Otherwise, they would lose their benefits.

Pam met with her clients and had some very enjoyable interactions. At the end of the year, Pam's clients completed satisfaction forms and praised her warm personality and caring attitude. However, when asked about their current status, none had a resume on file at the agency, some had not applied for any jobs, and only 50% had some kind of employment. Those who were not employed were devastated to hear that their benefits would stop. Pam was called into the manager's office when her stats were reviewed for contract compliance.

Judy also met with her clients and spent some time getting to know them; however, during the first meeting she advised them that they would be working toward concrete goals and let them know the consequences of failing to achieve these goals. One hundred percent of Judy's clients had a resume on file and had applied for at least three jobs per month. Moreover, 95% were employed at least part-time and the 5% who were not had documented health conditions. Based on Judy's satisfaction forms, clients rated her high for being warm and caring, and she also was rated high for helping them achieve their goals. Judy received an employee award for meeting agency targets and ensuring contract compliance.

In these two scenarios, we observe that sometimes a client may enjoy seeing their service provider and yet make little to no progress. Without defined goals, treatment approach, or time frames, a client may turn up for services every week and enjoy having an hour devoted to talking about their life, only to realize after two years that their life has not changed – they are still miserable at work, arguing with their spouse, and mired in debt. Likewise, if an employee does not know what outcomes they are to achieve, they may come to work every day, see clients and appear busy, and even get glowing reviews on client satisfaction surveys, yet fail to meet organizational goals. If an employee is unaware of the expectations, they may not only fail their clients, but also land the agency under a corrective action plan. Your agency expects you, as the supervisor, to ensure your organization's program goals are met, meaning your employees need to know what these goals are and how they are expected to achieve them.

Key Takeaways

- Ensure your direct reports have received written copies of organizational policies and procedures.
- Talk with your direct reports to clearly convey expectations and discuss any policies that may be pertinent for their role or department.

Setting Expectations 19

- Make sure employees understand any goals or objectives related to their position (e.g., target numbers, contracted client outcomes, etc.).
- Build a foundation for a healthy working alliance by asking your direct reports what they expect from you as well.

Discussion Questions

1. Does your team know what is expected of them? How can you make sure of this?
2. Have you ever asked your team what they expect from you?
3. Do team members have clear expectations for each other?

References

Buckingham, M., & Coffman, C. (1999). *First, break all the rules: What the world's greatest managers do differently*. New York: Simon and Schuster.

Constantino, M. J., Ametrano, R. M., & Greenberg, R. P. (2012). Clinician interventions and participant characteristics that foster adaptive patient expectations for psychotherapy and psychotherapeutic change. *Psychotherapy, 49*(4), 557–569. https://doi.org/10.1037/a0029440

Elliott, K. P., Westmacott, R., Hunsley, J., Rumstein-McKean, O., & Best, M. (2015). The process of seeking psychotherapy and its impact on therapy expectations and experiences. *Clinical Psychology & Psychotherapy, 22*(5), 399–408. https://doi.org/10.1002/cpp.1900

Hepworth, D. H., Rooney, R. H., Rooney, G. D., & Strom-Gottfried, K. (2017). *Direct social work practice: Theory and skills* (10th ed.). Boston, MA: Cengage Learning.

Maslow, A. H. (1943). A theory of human motivation. *Psychological Review, 50*(4), 370–396. https://doi.org/10.1037/h0054346

Miehls, D., Everett, J., Segal, C., & du Bois, C. (2013). MSW students' views of supervision: Factors contributing to satisfactory field experiences. *The Clinical Supervisor, 32*(1), 128–146. https://doi.org/10.1080/07325223.2013.782458

Neff, T. J., & Citrin, J. M. (2007). *You're in charge—Now what?* New York: Crown Publishing Group.

Weitkamp, K., Klein, E., Hofmann, H., Wiegand-Grefe, S., & Midgley, N. (2017). Therapy expectations of adolescents with depression entering psychodynamic psychotherapy: A qualitative study. *Journal of Infant, Child, and Adolescent Psychotherapy, 16*(1), 93–105. https://doi.org/10.1080/15289168.2016.1268883

Woodbury, D., Cohen, E., & Zayszly, J. (2001). *Excellence in supervision: Essential skills for the new supervisor*. Menlo Park: Course Technology Crisp.

3   Orienting and Onboarding

Once Upon a Time

At the beginning of my career, before I received my MSW, I took a volunteer position at a domestic violence shelter. After completing extensive training, I was assigned to co-facilitate a support group for women leaving violent relationships. The group met on Saturday mornings at a community center away from the shelter. The first Saturday I showed up, the building was locked and deserted. Women began to arrive, but my experienced co-facilitator was nowhere in sight. Eventually, a janitor walked by and offered to open up the room. I began to panic internally. I did not know the facility. I did not know the group roles or norms. In fact, I had never led a group before. Luckily, there was an experienced group member who helped orient me as well as three women who were there for the first time. Once everyone took a seat around the circle, they quickly began talking and the peer support aspect of the group took over. For the most part, I sat and observed. Miraculously, two of the three new women returned the following week. I never heard from the co-facilitator again. On the upside, I learned how to run a support group and felt appreciated by the group members who kept coming back. On the downside, I felt disregarded by the agency.

Two months later, the shelter director offered me a paid position as an overnight counselor. Eager to expand my social work experience, I jumped at the opportunity. I arrived early for my first overnight shift. The shelter was in a big, old building with several other businesses. Because it was a confidential location, there was no signage indicating where to go. I sat on a bench in the lobby, assuming someone would come and get me. As the minutes ticked by, I began to get worried (this was in the days before cell phones). It was late and I did not know the area, so I was reluctant to leave the building to find a pay phone. About ten minutes later, a woman exited the elevator and I asked if she knew who I was supposed to meet. Rushing out the door, she told me to go to the sixth floor. When I reached the sixth floor, a female security guard gave me a curious look and asked if I was a new resident. I told her I was a new hire and she led me to the back office. The staff member who was about to go off duty gave me a quick orientation (list of residents, quick review of possible issues, and directions to read the giant policy binder) and left. Thankfully, my first shift passed without incident. The relief person arrived the following morning at 7 a.m. and provided me with a very brief, very distracted tour. I left feeling ill-prepared and – once again – unappreciated. Needless to say, I did not work there for long. Having never forgotten how those experiences felt, I am always attentive to the importance of onboarding new staff and volunteers. First impressions mean a lot – not just your impression of the employee, but also their impression of you.

In contrast, when I arrived at the office for the first day of my MSW internship at a child protection agency, there was a banner in the lobby saying "Welcome MSW Interns." I was led into a room with coffee and pastries supplied by the intern field supervisors. I was walked around the building by my field instructor and introduced to everyone, shown the facilities, and oriented to the culture and norms of the workgroup. I was invited to join a group of staff for lunch and was encouraged to reach out to them with questions when my instructor was not available. Although I was given a policy manual to review (a common task for the new employee), I sat down feeling valued, enthusiastic, and eager to learn more about the organization and how I could excel in this work environment. I may be giving a little too much credit to this first day, but I went on to have a 15-year career at that same agency after graduation.

Overture

The first encounter with a client or an employee is when you begin to set the expectations described in the previous chapter. Their first impression of your office, your building, and most importantly of you sends a strong message about organizational values and how they can expect to be treated. If the fundamental task of the initial encounter is to establish a working relationship and set expectations (as covered in Chapters 1 and 2), then being thoughtful and purposeful about how to meet, greet, and orient your client or employee is critical. Once again, the parallels between the two processes will quickly become apparent.

The Micro Arena

How do you orient a new client? Perhaps you speak to them on the phone or send an email with detailed directions to your location. Maybe your building has a receptionist. If you work for a large organization, a design team may have developed processes to manage the flow of clients or customers, including the provision of explicit directions to explain eligibility criteria, payment criteria if applicable, and the steps clients must take to access your services. If you are a smaller operation, your organization has probably thought long and hard about providing a welcoming environment for clients, streamlining access to services, and considering details such as décor in the waiting room and access to restrooms.

It is difficult to fully prepare a client for everything that could occur in the course of therapy, during a stay in residential treatment, or while they are

22 Engagement

applying for public assistance. Nonetheless, direct service providers try to prepare clients as much as possible for what to expect.

In general, social service providers are trained to explain the nature of the helping process and to clarify that the relationship between social worker and client means working together to find solutions to the client's problems (Hepworth, Rooney, Rooney, & Strom-Gottfried, 2017). Social workers typically emphasize the importance of being open and honest, while acknowledging that the experience may at times be painful and could get worse before it gets better. They may introduce homework or activities the client needs to do between sessions as well as other areas of client responsibility such as keeping appointments or abiding by facility rules. In some settings, it is important to educate the client on what the service provider can and cannot do. This contract may be documented formally; other times, it is a verbal agreement reached during an individual or group orientation (Shulman, 2016).

Many clinical treatment approaches have very elaborate and specific orientations or preparations. Clinical interventions found to be most effective across a range of client problems in many different populations often include orientation and psychoeducation as the first stage of intervention. For example, Problem-Solving Therapy (PST) uses an "Orientation Checklist" (Hegel & Areán, 2002), including specific topics the therapist should cover during a first meeting (e.g., structure of the sessions, rationale for the treatment approach, normalizing problems, and describing all seven steps of the problem-solving process). Other commonly used treatment protocols with a defined orientation include Cognitive Behavioral Therapy (CBT), Trauma-Focused Cognitive Behavior Therapy (TFCBT), Eye Movement Desensitizing and Reprocessing (EMDR), Solution-Focused Brief Therapy (SFBT), and Brief Strategic Therapy. Amini and Woolley (2011) went so far as to develop a tool to measure therapist competency in the first session of Brief Strategic Therapy, noting that the first session is the most critical phase of the treatment model, as it "sets the stage for all subsequent therapeutic maneuvers" (p. 209). Other researchers have studied which types of orientation are most effective, cautioning against a reliance on video-taped orientations, which can be counterproductive (Johansen, Lumley, Cano, & Johansen, 2011). The bottom line is that a well-designed client introduction and socialization process is the underpinning of effective direct service delivery.

The Macro Arena

It is impossible to prepare your new employee for everything they may encounter at your workplace. Rago (2015) described attending a six-hour orientation for her field internship at a hospital to better understand her role in an interdisciplinary healthcare setting and know the essential skills of empathy, assessment, use of supervision, and self-care. Yet this comprehensive orientation could not prepare them for working with a Nepalese, non-English speaking family or distracting a toddler with toy trucks so the parents could attend to a very sick sibling. The infamous phrase "and other duties as assigned" – appearing at the end of nearly every job description – leaves the door open for any number of unanticipated tasks and activities that are required when working with complex people in complex systems. Nonetheless, a well-designed and well-executed new employee orientation pays off.

Based on a study of 264 new employees, Kammeyer-Mueller, Wanberg, Rubenstein, and Song (2013) found that the first 90 days are critical in building rapport with the organization, management, and colleagues. This finding was validated in a 2019 Jobvite survey of 1,500 American workers, which reported that 34% of respondents had left their job in the first 90 days (Jobvite, 2019). However, some employees will not even give you 90 days; the Wynhurst Group reported that 22% of staff turnover actually occurs in the first 45 days of employment (Maurer, 2015). This quick turnover can be costly, both in terms of dollars and lost productivity. Deloitte reported that the average US company spends around $4,000 and takes 52 days to hire a new employee (Garibaldi, 2016).

One way to reduce early turnover is through proper onboarding. The Wynhurst Group also noted that new employees who went through a structured onboarding program were 58% more likely to still be with their organization after three years (Maurer, 2015). The benefits of comprehensive onboarding go well beyond the initial employment period, leading to improved retention rates, time to productivity, and customer satisfaction (Aberdeen Group, 2006). Employees who receive quality onboarding report higher job satisfaction and organizational commitment (Maier & Brunstein, 2001).

In the business world, employee orientation (more so than the orientation of other stakeholder groups such as customers and shareholders) positively impacts corporate financial performance (de Bussy & Suprawan, 2012) and significantly influences workplace stress levels and turnover, especially when the supervisor is actively involved (Allee, 2012). New employee orientations (NEOs) are an effective method of socialization into the culture of the organization and are especially important if new hires or volunteers have limited exposure to the laws, ethics, values, and norms of the profession (Kim, Chai, Kim, & Park, 2015).

It is best to personally welcome your new employee on their first day rather than delegating the task to someone else – just as you would not have a client meet with a substitute therapist for their first session. For some organizations, this first encounter occurs following orientation by the HR or training department. For others, it may take place on the first day of employment with your company. Just like a new client, your new hire is nervous and excited and will respond very favorably to a warm greeting from someone who is not only expecting them, but is also delighted to meet them. Even if you are not the direct supervisor of this employee, you can still schedule an initial welcome meeting on their first day. As described in the previous chapter, your opportunity to enhance employee engagement and motivation starts the moment your new employee enters the front door of your agency.

24 *Engagement*

While the discussion so far has centered on people new to your organization, it is equally important to orient and train people who have been promoted to new positions within your organization (Watkins, 1992). In fact, part of the reason we are writing this book, and perhaps why you are reading it, is that far too often the assumption is that once oriented to a profession and an organization, the job is done. In addition to ongoing training, we encourage organizations to design and implement orientations specifically for employees who promote within the organization.

This Is How We Do It

A term often used interchangeably with onboarding is organizational socialization, or the process by which organizations help newcomers (or individuals moving to new organizational roles) acclimate to their work. Thinking of onboarding as organizational socialization is useful in designing a process to address how the organization functions, how to employ their skills in the new environment, and how to build relationships with their new colleagues. The following table covers the various dimensions of onboarding as well as the "what" and "why" behind each type.

Table 3.1

Dimension	What to Cover	Purpose
Organizational Onboarding	• Where to park • Where to eat and take breaks • Organizational history • Organizational philosophy and values • Common organizational acronyms	Understanding and adapting to the organizational culture
Technical Onboarding	• Employee handbook • Job description • Policies and procedures • Meeting schedule • Decision-making processes and lines of reporting • Available resources	Building self-efficacy in their new organization/role
Social Onboarding	• Team members and leaders • Key individuals throughout the organization • Key stakeholders outside the organization • Formal and informal social interactions	Creating a sense of community and belonging

Case Study

Quincy was the founder and director of Breaking Barriers, a small social service agency serving a low-income urban neighborhood. After five years of operating on a shoestring budget, the agency received a substantial grant from a local philanthropic organization to expand their geographical reach and develop services to address employment, parenting, and financial self-sufficiency needs for local residents. Quincy reached out to local universities to develop an internship program to provide additional individual and group counseling. With such rapid expansion underway, he hired an HR manager (Jill) and a program manager (Rueben) to help implement the new programming.

Jill and Rueben needed to hire multiple staff and recruit volunteers and interns. As they planned the onboarding process, they realized the complexity of hiring so many different classifications. They started by creating a new employee orientation for all new hires. This included a schedule that began with organizational onboarding and then branched out to technical and social onboarding depending on the employee assignment. Although they initially planned an in-person group orientation, Quincy pointed out that hiring would continue over time and they would not always have the resources to conduct an intensive orientation for one or two people at a time. He suggested they talk with an online educational company to see if they could develop learning modules for future employees.

The next step was to consider what on-the-job training would look like. They divided the job positions between them; Jill took the administrative staff and volunteers and Rueben took the outreach, social service, and counseling staff. They developed a job-training protocol including a matrix of core competencies for each position and a timeline for exposure to various experiences to help the employee develop and demonstrate these competencies. Quincy reviewed the plans to make sure everything was covered. To ensure a personal touch, he made a commitment to meet with every new employee in person during their first week on the job.

Pointing out how critical the first 90 days of employment are for new hires, Jill suggested they could maximize employee retention by ensuring new employees received close supervision during these first few months. In addition to weekly supervision, she recommended formal monthly reviews with all new hires using a checklist to monitor employee progress on developing knowledge and competencies in key aspects of their position.

The initial hiring period was a little rocky as Breaking Barriers implemented this new procedure. It took over a year to create online training modules and Jill and Rueben had to tweak their training plans. Despite the

26 *Engagement*

bumpy start, they experienced relatively low employee turnover. At exit interviews, Jill heard praise for their onboarding and orientation process.

Although a small agency with limited resources, Breaking Barriers prioritized employee onboarding and orientation. They knew that hiring and retaining staff in a challenging neighborhood, with less competitive salaries, and for an organization that was still growing and had an uncertain future would be challenging. But with a warm welcome, a focused new-hire training plan, and a high level of attention paid to new employees, they were able to recruit and retain many talented people.

Key Takeaways

- The first 90 days (perhaps even less) of your new hire's employment are crucial for retention.
- A structured onboarding program can help you retain new talent and reap long-term benefits for the organization and clients.
- Onboarding should cover three key dimensions: organizational, technical, and social.

Discussion Questions

1. Does your organization have a structured and consistent onboarding program?
2. To what extent does your organization's onboarding cover all three dimensions (organizational, technical, and social)?
3. What can you do to help your new hires feel welcomed and valued by the organization?
4. What actions can you take to help your new hires hit the ground running?

References

Aberdeen Group. (2006). *Onboarding benchmark report: Technology drivers help improve the new hire experience.* Retrieved January 22, 2020, from https://eitrainingcompany.com/wp-content/uploads/2012/04/10022007Extra_AberdeenReport.pdf

Allee, C. (2012). *New employee orientation: A survey of participant experiences and self-report outcomes* (Publication No. 3546786) [Doctoral dissertation, Chicago School of Professional Psychology]. ProQuest Dissertations Publishing.

Amini, R. L., & Woolley, S. R. (2011). First-session competency: The Brief Strategic Therapy Scale-1. *Journal of Marital and Family Therapy, 37*(2), 209–222. https://doi.org/10.1111/j.1752-0606.2010.00201.x

de Bussy, N. M., & Suprawan, L. (2012) Most valuable stakeholders: The impact of employee orientation on corporate financial performance. *Public Relations Review, 38*(2), 280–287. https://doi.org/10.1016/j.pubrev.2011.11.006

Garibaldi, A. A. (2016). *Talent analytics for dummies*. GlassDoor Publishing. Retrieve from https://resources.glassdoor.com/talent-analytics-for-dummies.html

Hegel, M., & Areán, P. A. (2002). *Problem-Solving Treatment for Primary Care (PST-PC): A treatment manual for depression*. Retrieved January 22, 2020, from http://dawncare.org/wp-content/uploads/2017/12/PST-PC-Manual.pdf

Hepworth, D. H., Rooney, R. H., Rooney, G. D., & Strom-Gottfried, K. (2017). *Direct social work practice: Theory and skills* (10th ed.). Boston, MA: Cengage.

Jobvite. (2019). *2019 job seeker nation survey*. Retrieve from https://web.jobvite.com/FY19_Website_2019JobSeekerNation_LP.html

Johansen, A. B., Lumley, M., Cano, A., & Johansen, A. (2011). Effects of video-based therapy preparation targeting experiential acceptance or the therapeutic alliance. *Psychotherapy, 48*(2), 163–169. https://doi.org/10.1037/a0022422

Kammeyer-Mueller, J., Wanberg, C., Rubenstein, A., & Song, Z. (2013). Support, undermining, and newcomer socialization: Fitting in during the first 90 days. *Academy of Management Journal, 56*(4), 1104–1124. https://doi.org/10.5465/amj.2010.0791

Kim, M., Chai, D. S., Kim, S., & Park, S. (2015). New employee orientation: Cases of Korean corporations. *Human Resource Development International, 18*(5), 481–498. https://doi.org/10.1080/13678868.2015.1079294

Maier, G. W., & Brunstein, J. C. (2001). The role of personal work goals in newcomers job satisfaction and organizational commitment: A longitudinal analysis. *Journal of Applied Psychology, 86*(5), 1034–1042. https://doi.org/10.1037/0021-9010.86.5.1034

Maurer, R. (2015, April 16). Onboarding key to retaining, engaging talent. *SHRM*. Retrieve from www.shrm.org/ResourcesAndTools/hr-topics/talent-acquisition/Pages/Onboarding-Key-Retaining-Engaging-Talent.aspx

Rago, S. (2015). Healthcare student social work orientation. *Field Educator, 5*(1), 1–3. http://fieldeducator.simmons.edu/article/healthcare-student-social-work-orientation

Shulman, L. (2016). *The skills of helping individuals, families, groups, and communities* (8th ed.). Boston, MA: Cengage.

Watkins, C. E., Jr. (1992). Reflections on the preparation of psychotherapy supervisors. *Journal of Clinical Psychology, 48*(1), 145–147. https://doi.org/cpdhkw

Part Two

Assessment

In clinical work, a good treatment/case plan is based on a thorough assessment, and the same is true in macro practice. While the information being gathered is very different, the ways in which you gather information for your assessment are much like those used to complete a client assessment. In this section, we will discuss how and what to observe (Chapter 4); how to apply interviewing skills to gather employee and workplace information (Chapter 4); and the role of formal and informal assessment tools to identify personality traits and communication styles to better know and understand how to work with your team (Chapter 5). Your team will be most productive if you have made a good assessment of their strengths and weaknesses and you can leverage individual skills, talents, and expertise for the benefit of the client, project or program, and the organization.

4   Observation

Once Upon a Time

I was a beginning case manager when I was asked to take a new employee with me on a home visit. The family we were visiting consisted of a mother with twin boys and an infant. The father was court ordered to stay away from the home due to a significant history of domestic violence. My role was to help the young mother find resources and support for her family. I gave the small apartment a cursory glance upon our arrival and settled into a chair next to the mother. I focused on listening to her story and demonstrating my very best interviewing skills to the new employee. I was impressed with my ability to engage the mother and assess her needs for employment, childcare, counseling, and so on. With a flourish, I reached in my bag and produced a list of resources to get her on the road to self-sufficiency. When we were done and back in the car, I asked the new employee about her impressions of the visit, expecting to hear how much she learned from watching the master at work. Instead, she described seeing a lock on the outside of the twins' bedroom, a man's shirt and shoes draped on a stool in the kitchen, and the mother coughing loudly to cover noises from the master bedroom. She ended by stating, "I think he's in the house and I don't believe that house is safe for those children." The new employee noticed all of this – I was so intently focused on talking that I noticed none of it. Based on her observations, I called the children's services social worker who made an unannounced visit and found the father in the home and the twin boys locked in their bedroom. The twins had several bruises that the family clearly did not want me to see. Fortunately, the baby was healthy. All three children were placed in temporary foster care while the mother went to a domestic violence shelter. She later told me that her husband had forced his way into the home three days before my visit. He told her to pretend everything was fine or he would put her in a wheelchair and make her watch while he did horrible things to the children. She was relieved that her children were finally safe. This was my first lesson in the power of observation, and I took it to heart.

Overture

The Greek philosopher Epictetus said, "We have two ears and one mouth so that we can listen twice as much as we speak." An updated version of this maxim from Mike Boyle is "You have two ears, two eyes, and one mouth. Use them

32   *Assessment*

in that order." As the previous story showed, too much focus on perfecting our verbal skills at the expense of our other senses can be dangerously negligent. In that situation, the verbal information was largely a distraction from the real issue, which could only be assessed via observation. The same applies once you are a supervisor or manager – you will learn more about your individual staff, your team, and your organization through observation than even the most well-crafted interview or survey. Of course, these latter two aspects are important and will be the focus of the next two chapters, but we purposefully put observation first so you will remember to gather data you can see, hear, and read.

The Micro Arena

As a direct service provider, you are well-trained at observation. Criteria in the 5th edition of the American Psychiatric Association's (2013) *Diagnostic and Statistical Manual of Mental Health Disorders* include behaviors or symptoms that have to be observed by the clinician, such as speech patterns or physical movements. When conducting a mental status exam, the clinician employs observation during the initial meeting when the client is telling their story and when answering questions, listing pertinent client observations such as appearance, posture, gestures, physical proximity and activity, behavior, and affect. Even if you are not a clinician, you likely engage in observation to help assess if your client is being truthful, sober, or cooperative.

One of the most common forms of documentation for client contact is the Subjective, Objective, Assessment, and Plan (SOAP) note. These are the core elements required as part of a case file for reimbursement or auditing purposes. While the "O" does not stand for observation, being objective certainly requires it. A client referred for mental health services by her infant son's pediatrician may verbally state that she is fine and does not need assistance, but the notes in the "O" section might state that the "client presented with flat affect, avoided eye contact, was dressed in soiled clothing, and did not respond to her infant when he cried." Such powers of observation are critical to making an accurate assessment of what might really be happening for the client and help guide next steps.

When working with a family, a critical part of the assessment is observing who sits next to whom, the presence or absence of physical contact or eye contact, and patterns of verbal and non-verbal interaction. When facilitating psychoeducational or process groups, the service provider scans the room to assess group functioning based on body posture, eye contact, who speaks when, who leads, who follows, and who retreats or avoids. This information is used to gauge family or group functioning and plan for interventions.

The Macro Arena

A good supervisor will use their powers of observation to gather data from the moment they enter the workplace. Observations are the first step to understanding the company culture. Schein and Schein's (2017) first level of analysis of organizational culture is the observation of artifacts, which they described as the aspects of a new group or culture that can be seen, heard, or felt. The authors specifically identified the physical environment, dress, observable rituals, and displays of emotion as ways to assess the "climate" of a workplace. Interestingly, the authors noted that while these visual artifacts are easy to observe, they are difficult to interpret, and they cautioned the observer to follow observation with questions to fully understand the meaning of observable phenomena (we will cover these in Chapter 7).

Observation in the workplace allows the supervisor or manager to see who is punctual and who is not, who takes breaks and when, who is present or absent, and what the workday flow of traffic is like. Being present in the office at different times is important to avoid a rigid schedule, as your staff are also watching you and may adapt to your schedule, either consciously or unconsciously keeping things from your view. As with families and groups, workgroup members often adopt certain roles such as leader, parent, child, clown, etc. You can use the same keen observation skills you used as a group facilitator or family therapist to gain insight into your team behavior and functioning, informing your approach when working with individuals and groups.

As with the home visit, the physical environment can provide information about an organization. Workplace design experts suggest that the physical workspace is an optimal opportunity to create a functional environment by considering dimensions such as rhythm, balance, proportion, equitability, flexibility, and unity (Rasmus, 2010). Fischer (2011) applied a psychosocial approach to the physical work environment, noting how the symbolic dimensions of the workspace provide an opportunity to examine the distribution of power and valued assets. Literature on requisite skills for culturally sensitive counseling has noted the need for multiculturally friendly offices, including guidance on specific design criteria and how this relates to psychotherapy outcomes (Benton & Overtree, 2012). This is another aspect of the workplace you can observe, assess, and consider as a target for intervention at the macro level.

In the field of human services, a considerable amount of the work your staff perform is not directly observable by you. While you can do things like job shadowing and scheduled and unscheduled rounds to create opportunities for observation, you cannot accompany your employees during every client session, home visit, or group. If you cannot directly witness your employee carrying out their job duties, you can gather information by observing the quantity, quality, and timeliness of their work employing interviews (Chapter 5), and using assessment measures (Chapter 6). Regardless of how you are gathering information, you should document your observations. As with client documentation, your observations should be behavioral and specific. Your employee documentation should also be balanced to include positives as well as areas for improvement.

We encourage you to create opportunities to observe your employees doing their work, as you will gain a far more accurate assessment of their strengths and opportunities for development. One of the authors of this book attended a conference training session that included Dr. Marion Bogo, a social work scholar whose research has focused on the training of social work students. Dr. Bogo described a student interview with a simulated client and when

34 *Assessment*

asked after the interview what the most difficult part of the client interaction was, the student described feeling sad when the client started crying as they talked about the death of a close relative. The student explained how she leaned in toward the client to make it clear she was really listening and then handed the client a tissue for her tears. However, those observing the interview saw that the student had actually leaned back from the client, appeared distressed, and took a tissue to blow her own nose. The student had genuinely thought she had done as she described. This scenario is likely very common when employees recount their actions when providing services – not with an intent to be dishonest, but rather with a rose-tinted memory, so to speak. Use of video or audio recording (with appropriate employee and client consent) or even peer observation can be a substitute for direct observation and, within a trusting supervisory relationship, employees will hopefully embrace this as an opportunity to grow and develop as practitioners.

This Is How We Do It

The following table provides some suggestions for what to observe in different dimensions of the workplace.

Table 4.1

Dimension	What to Observe	Purpose
Work Environment	• What is the condition of the building and furnishings? • Are there gathering spaces for staff? • Is the office quiet or lively? • Does the environment seem warm and welcoming or cold and impersonal?	Understanding the organizational culture Assessing how well the workplace design contributes to employee and client outcomes Seeing how clients, community partners, or new employees experience your agency
Worker Appearance and Behavior	• Are people dressed formally or casually? • Do people seem relaxed or stressed? • Are people punctual or usually running late? • Who are the significant cliques or dyads? • Do certain staff seem isolated from the others?	Understanding the organizational culture Assessing individual and team functioning Determining areas for support or development
Work Product	• What is the worker's quantity of work as compared to expectations? • Does the worker meet their deadlines? • Is paperwork free from errors? • What do colleagues say about the worker? • What feedback has been received from the worker's clients?	Identifying issues to address Identifying areas for praise or recognition

Case Study

Omar called his first team meeting as a new manager. Marcus, the most senior team member, arrived early and sat at the opposite end of the table facing Omar. Dressed in a suit and tie, he placed his notebook and pen on the table, ready for business. Jody, another longstanding team member, arrived next. She was dressed casually and was eating cereal from a plastic bowl. She scanned the room and selected a seat far from Marcus. The two of them did not make eye contact or say a word to each other. Jane and Margot arrived together, also dressed casually, talking to one another quietly, absorbed in their conversation. They sat next to each other and continued chatting, not acknowledging anyone else in the room. Joseph, one of the newest supervisors, arrived carrying case files and talking on his Bluetooth. He had a neatly trimmed beard and was wearing smart slacks and a collared shirt. He smiled and nodded to folks around the table as he finished his call. There was one empty seat. Jamie, the clinical director, had not called in or left any messages for Omar, so he asked if anyone knew when she would arrive. Marcus rolled his eyes and stated that she was always late and the group should not wait for her. Marcus looked at Jane and Margot and put his finger on his lips to shush them and bring the meeting to order.

The behavior of Omar's team members upon arrival provided him with rich information to consider as he began to assess his new workgroup. Some things were easily recognizable, such as Marcus' perception of himself as a leader and Jane and Margot's apparent deference to him. Other observations required further exploration. For example, was there a dress code, and, if so, were any individuals exempt? Or did Marcus and Joseph have other meetings or appointments that would require more formal attire? Jody's behavior suggested that she did not care for Marcus, which Omar would have to explore further. In just the first five minutes, Omar had gathered a wealth of data to continue to mull over as he plunged into his first meeting.

Key Takeaways

- Observation is an extremely valuable management skill.
- When you cannot observe your employee directly, evaluate their output and the quality of their work.
- When the work performance is significant, make sure to document it.
- Documentation should be specific and behavioral.
- Be sure to document positives as well as areas for improvement.

36 *Assessment*

Discussion Questions

1. How can you increase your opportunities to observe the work of your staff?
2. Do you take note of positive performance or only focus on performance problems?
3. Think of your recent interactions with staff. Can you recall people's body language, facial expressions, and tone of voice?
4. Is your smartphone use hindering your ability to observe your staff and surroundings?

References

American Psychiatric Association. (2013). *Diagnostic and statistical manual of mental disorders* (DSM-5®). https://doi.org/10.1176/appi.books.9780890425596

Benton, J. M., & Overtree, C. E. (2012). Multicultural office design: A case example. *Professional Psychology: Research and Practice, 43*(3), 265–269. https://doi.org/10.1037/a0027443

Fischer, G.-N. (2011). *Individuals and environment: A psychosocial approach to workspace.* Berlin: De Gruyter.

Rasmus, D. W. (2010). *Management by design: Applying design principles to the work experience.* Hoboken, NJ: John Wiley & Sons.

Schein, E. H., & Schein, P. (2017). *Organizational culture and leadership* (5th ed.). Hoboken, NJ: John Wiley & Sons.

5 Interviewing

Once Upon a Time

My first assignment at Child Protective Services was as an initial investigator. As referrals of child abuse and neglect came into the Child Abuse Hotline, they were distributed to the investigators and required a response of three hours, three days, or ten days depending on the level of severity. Despite having just received my MSW with a specialty in public child welfare and six weeks of extensive training, I was far from an expert at interviewing. During the first few weeks, I clung to my "cheat sheets" – lists of questions and prompts to remind me what to ask. I was extremely stilted in my approach, walking through a list of questions, anxious not to forget anything. I soon realized this was not working. Putting away the question list, I shifted to a more client-centered approach by listening empathically and letting the client lead the conversation. I began to get a lot more information and came back to the office excited to share with my supervisor all the details I had learned. But far too often, while I learned a lot about the client and their life history, I did not necessarily have the information needed to determine the children's safety. During this period, I had to make many repeat visits to ask follow-up questions that I had failed to explore the first time around. Over time, I developed a style that incorporated both approaches, ensuring the people I interviewed felt heard and cared about while allowing me to gather the critical information needed to determine the children's safety and well-being as well as assess the family's needs.

Overture

In a clinical context, interviewing is used to collect data to formulate a diagnosis or flesh out the presenting problem and drive the treatment plan. In an administrative context, interviewing typically refers to when candidates are asked questions to determine their fit for a position in the organization. While interviewing job candidates is important, it will not be the focus of this chapter. Instead, we will discuss how you can use your well-honed clinical interviewing skills to gather the information you need to carefully and accurately diagnose organizational issues. As with clinical practice, the client (in this case, the

38   *Assessment*

employee, workgroup, or key stakeholder) usually knows the problem best and has the wisdom to find the best solution; your job is to facilitate this problem identification and problem-solving process.

The Micro Arena

The initial clinical interview usually features an agenda depending on the agency context and services provided. During the first meeting, the worker establishes whether there is a need for services; gathers information to determine what resources, intervention, or service delivery medium will best serve the client; and determines next steps. In a hospital, the interview may be focused on discharge planning. In child protective services, the interview is used to determine child safety and protection and gather critical data to drive the decision-making process. In substance abuse treatment, the intake interview explores factors such as frequency, severity, and type of substance use as well as the client's readiness for treatment to establish the most suitable setting for treatment services. Sometimes the interview is brief and focused on establishing eligibility and other times several meetings are needed to develop a comprehensive picture of the client's needs and strengths as well as to establish a baseline of data to measure future progress. The first interview can also be an intervention, representing the only opportunity the service provider has to try and help the client, although in other cases it is anticipated as the beginning of a long-term relationship between service provider and service recipient.

As the primary source of data for the biopsychosocial clinical assessment, the client interview is the cornerstone of what we do when working directly with clients. The clinical interview is more than a conversation – it is the beginning phase of problem solving that takes place in the context of a relationship, where mutually agreed upon goals, derived from a joint understanding of the facts, are established (Kadushin & Kadushin, 2013). A practitioner cannot create a case plan until they have made an assessment of the client system based on carefully gathered facts. Gathering these facts requires the application of clinical knowledge and skills including reflection, clarification, questioning, interpretation, confrontation, activation, education, and information-giving. The clinician asks for clarification and specific examples in an effort to avoid taking information at face value and missing critical facts a client might wish to conceal for various reasons. Clinicians also know the value of reflecting on their biases to ensure they do not jump to conclusions or fall prey to countertransference responses. They are trained to be culturally aware and avoid the lure of stereotypes. These very ingredients will serve you well as a supervisor and manager. This same process, adapted to the situation in front of you in the form of an underperforming employee, a disgruntled community member, or a dysfunctional team or workgroup, will ensure you conduct a thorough assessment of the facts while engaging the person or group in a positive interaction aimed at clarifying the problem at hand and identifying the resources needed to find a solution.

The Macro Arena

While many clinical interviewing skills will serve you well when interviewing potential employees to hire, the majority of "interviews" with your staff, team members, or stakeholders will be more generally labeled as meetings. Often, the initial meeting between you and an employee will be a time when you will collect information to best assess the employee's needs and strengths and begin to formulate ideas about the best approach for supervision and coaching in the future. Other meetings that fall into this category include performance reviews or performance improvement meetings. However, engaging your interviewing skills in the supervisory and management context can extend beyond these defined interactions, greatly enhancing your ability to proactively identify problems and solutions during regular employee conferences, team meetings, and ad hoc committee meetings. You do not need to be the leader or chair of these meetings to apply interviewing techniques (e.g., listening, reflecting, clarifying, summarizing, and questioning) and move your team in a positive direction. Later in this book, we will go into greater detail on how to specifically apply the interviewing skills associated with MI (Chapter 8), PST (Chapter 9), and SF Therapy (Chapter 9) as a macro practitioner.

The macro practice literature uses different names for familiar clinical practices. For example, Appreciative Inquiry ([AI]; Cooperrider & Whitney, 2005) uses terms to describe the five stages of the employee interview, which clearly align with clinical interview objectives. The first stage of AI, "definition," is akin to the first question of any clinical encounter ("what brings you here today?"); from there, the manager moves on to problem definition. The next stage, "discovery," engages the employee or team in storytelling to help them get to know one another. This stage is where the bulk of general information and background is shared. In the third stage, the AI "dream" can be regarded as the "miracle question" where the employee or team imagines what it will be like when the problem is solved. Next, the AI "design" stage refers to the setting of mutually agreed upon goals. AI ends with the "destiny" stage, which involves the plan of action drawn up at the end of the meeting. We hope you can see that, although this may be the first time you are reading about AI, you already know how to do the tasks associated with these stages and have likely done them many times before.

Other more general management texts attempting to guide managers on employee appraisal meetings or coaching sessions have described how to apply skills that are almost identical to those used in a clinical interview. For example, Wilson's (2014) performance coaching book devotes three chapters

40   *Assessment*

on how to listen, reflect, clarify and summarize, and question, with step-by-step skill development activities and case examples. Kirkpatrick and Grote's (2006) popular management book on employee performance improvement, appraisal, and coaching covers basics such as being prepared, avoiding interruptions, establishing rapport, explaining purpose, encouraging the employee to talk, listening, identifying strengths, and focusing on the future. Again, these are all things any good clinician, case manager, or counselor already knows and does daily. Even the meeting objectives are familiar: to agree on the performance issue, identify strengths and areas for improvement, agree on an improvement plan, and determine what needs to be done before the next meeting.

This is again a time where it is pertinent to note that while you are employing clinical skills and techniques, you are not taking on the role of a clinician. Remember that your interview is not designed to elicit information needed to ascertain an employee's psychiatric diagnosis or mental health issues. Instead, it is best to maintain focus on behaviors observed in the workplace that enhance or inhibit optimal work performance. As a supervisor, your goal is to gather information so you can assess your employees' performance and ensure quality service delivery for clients; as a manager, your aim is to gather information about the workplace and community your organization serves to ensure your agency is mission driven and is striving to achieve organizational goals.

The information you gather is only part of the value of your interview – further value is generated from relationship-building between you and your employees. By asking questions and listening to the responses, you are demonstrating empathy to your employees. Perceived empathy from a supervisor enhances counselor learning (Payne & Gralinski, 1968) and is positively correlated to moderating employee stress levels resulting from difficult clients (Richard, Bupp, & Alzaidalsharief, 2016). Supervisors who are viewed as good listeners have been shown to enhance job satisfaction and improve employee performance (Lloyd, Boer, & Voelpel, 2015).

This Is How We Do It

The Focused-Conversation Method developed by the Institute of Cultural Affairs is a favorite of one of the authors of this book. It is a structured process that uses four types of questions that take the conversation from the superficial level to deeper understanding: objective, reflective, interpretive, and decisional. The manager facilitates the conversation, moving through each type in order and asking a single question or multiple questions depending on the subject and purpose of the discussion. The method works well with individuals and groups in a variety of settings. The following table below presents one method that can be applied when talking with an employee with performance issues.

Interviewing 41

Table 5.1

Component	What to Ask	Purpose
Objective	• What have you been working on recently? • What deadlines are you aware you have missed? • What happened from your point of view? • What can you tell me about what's been happening with your work?	Beginning with data, facts, and external reality Drawing out observable data about the subject
Reflective	• How do you feel about the work you do? • What has been most difficult for you in your work? • Where have you experienced pressure or frustration? • What part might I have played in causing this situation?	Evoking personal reactions, internal responses, and associations
Interpretive	• What would you say are the underlying issues behind these difficulties? • How have you noticed that other people deal with these difficulties? • What practical means could we take to enable you to complete your work on time?	Drawing out meaning, values, significance, and implications
Decisional	• What would it take to help you apply what you learned? • What can you and I do to make sure your job is done effectively? • What is the first action we need to take? • When can you and I meet again and check signals on these decisions?	Bringing the discussion to a close, eliciting resolution, and solidifying decisions moving forward

Case Study

Margarita was a program manager in a counseling clinic serving severely mentally ill clients. A critical incident occurred at the clinic with a client who was decompensating. The client came into the office on a day when he was not scheduled and wanted to see his therapist. The reception-ist informed him that his therapist was at lunch and would be back in

42   *Assessment*

30 minutes. He took a seat in the lobby but became increasingly agitated. After ten minutes, he began pacing and ranting. When the receptionist could not get him to calm down, she left her station to find someone to help. While she was gone, the client began throwing furniture and tried to break down the door leading to the counseling offices. The receptionist called 911 and the police arrived and took the client to the psychiatric hospital where he was placed on a 48-hour hold. While no one was injured in the incident, it was extremely traumatizing for the staff and clients who were in the office at the time.

Margarita was out of town on the day of the incident. While interviewing people for the incident report upon her return, she received varying accounts of what happened. It soon became clear that staff members were pointing the finger at each other for failing to prevent the incident. Margarita scheduled an all-staff meeting for the clinic and used the focused-conversation method to design the discussion. She began with *objective* questions: What happened on the day of the incident? What did you see or hear? If you were in the office, what did you do during the incident? She then moved to *reflective* questions: What feelings did you experience? What was most frightening? What was surprising? Next came *interpretive* questions: Why do you think this happened? What might have been some other contributing factors? How do you think this has impacted our staff and clients? What can we learn from this? She finished with *decisional* questions: How can we be supportive to the people who were in the office that day? What should we do differently as a result of this incident? How will this impact our work going forward?

In the course of the conversation, staff had an opportunity to share their experiences and feelings. Margarita listened and summarized what she heard to be sure she understood everyone's perspective. The team was then able to identify strategies to help prevent future incidents from occurring.

Key Takeaways

- Your clinical skills of listening, reflecting, clarifying, summarizing, and questioning can be used effectively in your role as a supervisor or manager.
- While you are not your staff's clinician, you should apply the same level of attentiveness, self-reflection, and cultural awareness as you would with clients.
- Asking questions and listening demonstrates empathy, which in turn can enhance employee learning, performance, and satisfaction.
- Four types of questions can help you to gather information and find solutions more effectively: objective, reflective, interpretive, and decisional.

Discussion Questions

1. When your employees come to you with problems, how often do you tell them what to do vs. asking questions to help them figure it out for themselves?
2. Do you employ a variety of questions with your staff?
3. Do your staff see you as empathetic? How do you know?

References

Cooperrider, D. L., & Whitney, D. (2005). *Appreciative inquiry: A positive revolution in change.* San Francisco, CA: Berrett-Koehler.

Kadushin, A., & Kadushin, D. (2013). *The social work interview.* New York: Columbia University Press.

Kirkpatrick, D. L., & Grote, R. (2006). *Improving employee performance through appraisal and coaching* (2nd ed.). New York: American Management Association.

Lloyd, K. J., Boer, D., & Voelpel, S. C. (2015). From listening to leading: Toward an understanding of supervisor listening within the framework of leader-member exchange theory. *International Journal of Business Communication, 54*(4), 431–451. https://doi.org/10.1177/2329488415572778

Payne, P. A., & Gralinski, D. M. (1968). Effects of supervisor style and empathy upon counselor learning. *Journal of Counseling Psychology, 15*(6), 517–521. https://doi.org/10.1037/h0026255

Richard, E. M., Bupp, C. P., & Alzaidalsharief, R. G. (2016). Supervisor empathy moderates the negative effects of customer injustice. In N. E. Ashkanasy, C. E. J. Härtel, & W. J. Zerbe (Eds.), *Emotions and organizational governance research on emotion in organizations* (Vol. 12, pp. 117–140). Bingley: Emerald Publishing Limited. https://doi.org/10.1108/s1746-979120160000012004

Wilson, C. (2014). *Performance coaching: A complete guide to best practice coaching and training* (2nd ed.). London: Kogan Page.

6   Assessment Tools

Once Upon a Time

When I started as a clinician in an outpatient clinic providing therapy to children and youth, I was surprised to discover that the agency required children and their caretakers to complete a battery of tests, such as the Child Behavior Checklist, the Beck Depression Inventory, Post-traumatic Stress Disorder Checklist, etc. At first, I resented the intrusion of these tests during the rapport building phase, as they seemed impersonal and I worried they would interfere with client engagement. To my surprise, most clients were fairly compliant and seemed relieved to have a way to share information in this way. One foster mother said that it really helped to catalog the behaviors she observed and to realize that other children must have similar problems. Children shared information on the checklist that they would likely not bring up so early in treatment, but since I had read their responses it could be incorporated into treatment planning earlier in the process. They repeated the tests at the three- and six-month marks and now we had documented evidence of their progress. We could see areas of improvement and areas needing additional work. All of this could be incorporated into goal setting and treatment planning.

As a new supervisor, it did not occur to me that a similar approach could be applied when working with staff. One of my first "Aha!" moments in this regard was when I attended a training on communication and took the Myers-Briggs test. I always knew I was extroverted, but I had not really considered how that might be experienced by my staff, especially those who were introverted. I began to adapt my communication style, providing agendas ahead of time and creating opportunities for everyone to share their thoughts through various media. I also had a new lens through which to interpret others' behavior. My quiet staff were not (necessarily) uninterested; rather, they were (more likely) introverted. Then, I was introduced to the Gallup 12 questions (Q12) and StrengthsFinder assessment. My entire team was assessed via the Q12 and I could see where I needed to improve and develop a plan to increase my scores in trouble spots. We posted our top five strengths and used this knowledge to guide our work, from task assignment and team composition to praise and recognition. We used the strengths in quarterly reviews to create professional development goals. It gradually dawned on me: just as in clinical practice, I was collecting data to increase self-awareness, better understand employee behavior, and assess the level of functioning of a workgroup, and I was using this data to create plans to improve performance, both my own and that of my team members.

Overture

Many of us are interested in understanding human behavior and categorizing personality types and tendencies. Our interest is fueled by the proliferation of surveys that claim to provide a label representing a cluster of common characteristics often found on self-help bookshelves and across social media. While many of these have little scientific merit (What breed of dog are you? Take this Facebook quiz and find out!), psychologists have produced a number of empirically validated measures to assess human behavior and personality, and many of these diagnostic tests have become part of a routine battery of assessments used in clinical practice. Similarly, assessment measures are becoming increasingly popular in organizations to better understand employee behavior and guide management practices. Numerous tools are available to assess organizational capacity (Informing Change, 2017) as well as assessments of employee behaviors (e.g., Dominance, Influence, Steadiness, and Compliance (DISC); StrengthsFinder; and Myers-Briggs). Moreover, individual assessments can help employees increase self-awareness, self-regulation, and performance, guiding supervisors and managers on how to more effectively coach staff and build teams.

The Micro Arena

Regardless of your practice setting, it is critical to conduct some form of assessment when working with clients in order to select the best intervention. Unless you are in private practice, you have likely relied on the tools your agency provided, as described in the opening story of this chapter. Psychologists may use projective tests such as the Rorschach or the Thematic Apperception Test (TAT) along with objective tests such as the Minnesota Multiphasic Personality Inventory (MMPI). Social workers may use assessment tools including a genogram or an ecomap to better understand family and community relationships. In certain settings, risk assessments or screening tools are employed to assess the frequency, severity, and chronicity of the social or emotional problems of the client or patient. These tools help practitioners efficiently gather comprehensive information that has either been demonstrated through research or determined through practice to be pertinent when identifying the type and level of intervention. An added benefit is that use of formal assessments not only informs the practitioner about the presenting problems, prognosis, and potential treatment alternatives, but can also enhance service adherence and prevent premature termination (Gastaud, Feil, Merg, & Nunes, 2014).

46 *Assessment*

Formal assessment tools are also important to determine if what we are doing is actually working. All too often in human services, we tend to rely on doing what feels right subjectively rather than doing what we can demonstrate to be effective objectively. The focus on evidence-based treatments and data-driven practice has largely been in response to the discovery that many interventions we felt good about did not actually achieve the desired results.

Human service agencies use any number of metrics to measure client outcomes as a requirement of grant funding or insurance reimbursements. As research has confirmed (e.g., Lambert, 2010), good clinicians know that measuring the presence of symptoms and monitoring symptom relief and behavior change increases client engagement and satisfaction and helps prevent premature dropout. Non-clinical service providers also use outcome data to ensure their programs are helping people as intended, whether it be by finding shelter, employment, maintaining sobriety, or achieving case-plan goals. In either setting, measuring outcomes relies on collecting baseline data via an initial assessment and periodically checking to see if this data changes over time.

Several tools have been developed (and have a growing evidence base) to continually assess and monitor client symptoms and progress in treatment. Although initially developed for work with children and adolescents as part of the Managing and Adapting Practice (MAP) system (Kataoka et al., 2014), clinical dashboards using Excel spreadsheets track assessment measures and interventions and visually present progress (or lack of progress) for both practitioner and client to see. Another tool used to assess and monitor client outcomes and the helping relationship is Feedback Informed Treatment (FIT; Tilsen & McNamee, 2014). FIT provides tools for both adults and children that can be used to routinely and formally solicit feedback from service recipients. The Outcome Rating Scale (ORS) assesses the client's progress through ratings of psychological functioning and distress, whereas the Session Rating Scale (SRS) assesses the client's perception of the client-therapist alliance. As with the clinical dashboard, this information is used to tailor service delivery and make adjustments in order to maximize treatment effects.

Despite the wide availability of tests and surveys, some practitioners forgo formal assessment tools unless required as part of agency policy or reimbursement criteria. This is surprising considering the extensive evidence that using assessment and monitoring tools can significantly improve treatment outcomes (Lambert & Harmon, 2018). Kirchner, Marshall, and Poyner (2017) even found that mandated use of suicide assessment tools significantly reduced attempted and completed suicides.

Various explanations for resistance to assessment tools have been generated, including lack of time and resources, suspicion of management motives, financial and training burden, and lack of staff buy-in (Boswell, Kraus, Miller, & Lambert, 2015). Another barrier especially critical to confront as a supervisor or manager is that tools used to track client and therapist progress may expose the practitioner's vulnerabilities (Lambert & Harmon, 2018). This could be especially daunting if social workers, therapists, and other human service providers are hired and fired based solely on objectively measured client outcome measures (Silver Wolf, 2018). However, ethical practice demands we put this fear to the side and embrace the value of assessment and monitoring tools, as they are a proven method to enhance positive outcomes for clients.

The Macro Arena

As a supervisor or manager, it is less likely that you will require your employees to take formal assessment tests. While it is rare, some organizations use the MMPI as a screening tool. In Los Angeles County, for example, child protective service workers are required to take the MMPI as part of a psychological evaluation prior to hiring and, depending on the results may be ruled out as a potential candidate. If you are considering the use of personality testing as a pre-employment screening tool, we recommend you get acquainted with the employment laws for your state and consider relevant ethical and cultural considerations. It is especially important that the tests are not used to discriminate against an applicant based on a protected classification and that privacy rights are safeguarded (Youngman, 2017).

For the most part, personality tests are used as a team building tool or incorporated as part of a communication or leadership training. Some organizations invest in a particular tool as part of their training budget (e.g., StrengthsFinder or DISC). Depending on the available funds and leadership buy-in, the application of the assessment results may be incorporated into performance reviews, used to create balanced teams, and provide a shared vernacular to build team cohesion. If budgets are tight or leadership is not supportive, supervisors and managers can find various online surveys (although caution should be taken in selecting these and due diligence should be applied in researching their validity and reliability). Some organizations conduct 360-degree employee assessments where they measure a set of competencies, broken down into behaviors, and ask various team members (e.g. peers, supervisor, and direct reports) to rate the employee on these behaviors. While the results of such assessments are by nature subjective, using 360-degree assessments has been shown to support organizational and behavior change (Bracken & Rose, 2011) as well as promote organizational justice (Karkoulian, Assaker, & Hallak, 2016). In much the same way as client test results and survey responses are used to guide treatment planning, the results of workplace surveys can be used to assign tasks, develop supervisory strategies, and identify individualized approaches to achieve performance objectives.

Most work today is done as part of a team and this is particularly true of human services organizations. Kendall and Salas (2004) recommended five types of measures that can help assess team functioning: event-based measurement, performance monitoring, behaviorally anchored rating scales, behavioral observation scales, and self-report measures. Arguably the most well-known assessment of group functioning that can be applied to teams is the five-stage concept based on the theory originally developed by Bruce Tuckman in the

48   *Assessment*

1970s (Tuckman & Jensen, 1977). Whether a workgroup is forming, storming, norming, performing, or adjourning can often be assessed informally from observation of group interactions and dynamics (in fact, if you have recently moved into your team's leadership position, you may have changed your team's stage of development – changes in team composition can do that; Peralta, Lourenço, Lopes, Baptista, & Pais, 2018). Much like a psychotherapy group, support group, or classroom, a combination of informal and formal assessments can help you identify the group's developmental stage and level of functioning and provide guidance on how to facilitate growth and achieve group goals.

Organizational assessments largely ask whether the agency is meeting expected standards. As a supervisor or manager, it is unlikely you will have to complete an organizational diagnosis, but you should be aware of the organization's vision, mission, and goals and the role that your team or workgroup plays in meeting these goals. You can then benchmark performance based on achievement of assigned goals and objectives and use any number of project management and data visualization tools to track change over time. Using this data to adapt behavior as needed will help ensure you have high performing individuals, teams, and organizations.

Lastly, there are self-assessments and surveys to evaluate your own supervisory, management, and leadership style and identify areas for growth and development. For example, Northouse's (2013) book on leadership walks the reader through many of the predominant theories of leadership style, with each chapter concluding with a version of a survey related to the theory. Each survey or quiz provides an opportunity to reflect on your own practice and approach to supervision and leadership as well as identify areas of strength and areas for growth. Not every agency has the resources or motivation to engage in assessment and ongoing evaluation of their staff and leadership team, but there is nothing to stop you from doing this work yourself.

Many formal assessment tools are at your disposal at little to no cost and can be incorporated into retreats, trainings, or team building meetings. Informal tools can be adapted from both the management literature (e.g., 360-degree assessments) and from clinical practice (e.g., FIT). Regardless of your resources, you should build a dashboard of critical performance measures for your team and track them regularly, providing regular reports to your team on their progress and brainstorming as a group when you may need to change course or consider new approaches when targets are not met.

This Is How We Do It

There are a variety of standardized assessment tools you can use for assessing your staff and team. The following list is not comprehensive by any means, but it is a good place to start if you are considering the use of assessments in your role as a manager. Also, keep in mind that some of the individual assessments could be used as team assessments if all members take them and you share and discuss the results as a team.

Assessment Tools 49

Table 6.1

Type	Assessment Tool	Description
Individual Assessments	Gallup's StrengthsFinder 2.0	Each person's top 5 strengths
	360-Degree Assessment	Multi-rater feedback from a variety of stakeholders including self-assessment
	DISC	Personality and behavior profile
	Myers-Briggs Type Indicator	Sorts individuals into 16 personality types
	Maslach Burnout Inventory	Measure of occupational burnout
Team Assessments	Stages of Team Development	Group cohesiveness and productivity
	Competing Values Assessment	Assess organizational culture on two axes: flexibility vs. control and internal vs. external
	Belbin's Team Roles	What each person contributes to the team
	Z Process	A person's role preference when working on a team

Case Study

After working for two years as an employment specialist at a large community-based agency, Ashley was promoted to supervisor at a program site in a different region. She was acquainted with some of her new supervisees from past agency trainings but had not worked closely with them. Because Ashley had excelled as an employment specialist, she felt confident in her ability to oversee her team's day-to-day work, but she wanted to know more about them so she could be an effective leader for the team.

Her first task was to spend some time in the management information system (MIS), reviewing key data points such as caseload size and distribution, average number of cases opened and closed per month, time to employment, and type of employment. Ashley then drilled down to the individual level to see how each employee performed on key performance indicators that were required for the county contract and aligned with the agency vision and mission. She scheduled individual meetings with each employee and created a list of questions to get to know each individual and obtain pertinent information about their work habits, strengths, weaknesses, and goals.

Having previously worked at a child mental health clinic, Ashley had been introduced to FIT, and so she took a few questions from this tool and added them to her supervision questions. When she met with her staff for the first time, she let them know that at the beginning of each supervision session, she was going to ask them to rate their current workplace well-being (e.g., work performance, job satisfaction, workplace relationships, and level of workplace stress) and she would plot their scores on a chart. At the end of each meeting, she would also ask them to rate their meeting together based on four factors related to their working alliance (e.g., feeling heard and understood, addressed issues of concern, and supervisory style). Ashley let them know that this would provide valuable feedback on how to best support them. While some of the staff found this approach unusual, she asked them to try it for a few weeks to see how it felt.

Her first meetings went very well, as she began to get a good sense of the team and to consider what approach might best work for each employee. After Ashley completed a self-assessment survey that showed a tendency toward an achievement-oriented style, she identified that some of her staff needed a more supportive touch, such as a new staff person who directly stated they were feeling insecure and would like more direction.

During meetings, Ashley watched group dynamics and observed that during the first two meetings, everyone was polite, answered questions, and worked through the agenda briskly (norming). However, by the third meeting, tension emerged when several team members expressed frustration with management for introducing new documentation procedures. While Ashley felt defensive and was about to justify the policies, she recognized the team was moving into another phase (storming) and that this was a good sign. They were beginning to trust her enough to complain. She listened, took notes, and reflected back and summarized their concerns. She thanked them for bringing these issues to her attention and suggested they tackle them one by one as a team at future meetings.

A couple of months later, Ashley approached her manager to get support for holding a team retreat. While she felt good about the progress her team was making, she knew they were struggling to keep up with increased caseloads and it was impacting morale. Ashley wanted to hold a four-hour offsite retreat with an outside facilitator, and to purchase books and a self-assessment survey for her team. She shared her rationale and goals for the retreat and presented data on her team to help make her case. Ashley's manager was supportive but concerned about the limited training budget. After some discussion, they agreed to use the conference room onsite and Ashley's manager said she would cover the cost of the books and assessment. Ashley contacted a former colleague who agreed to facilitate the retreat for a reduced rate. The retreat was a great success. Team members learned about each other's communication styles and engaged in activities to help them leverage one another's strengths. They developed a creative plan to help them better manage their high caseloads and ended the morning by creating team goals and metrics.

Within just three months on the job, Ashley had learned about the team – and herself as a leader – through the use of both formal and informal assessment tools and had used this process to engage her staff (and her manager) and to develop mutually agreed upon goals. In addition, she had established benchmarks and a process to systematically collect data on her team's performance, the individual performance of each team member, and her own performance as a supervisor. Ashley was well on her way to becoming a highly effective leader.

Key Takeaways

- Formalized assessments can help staff increase self-awareness, self-regulation, and performance.
- Staff or team assessments can be repeated over time to gauge progress and identify areas for improvement.
- Your skills of observation and interviewing are also powerful assessment tools.

Discussion Questions

1. What stage of team development is your team in? How can you move them to the next stage?
2. Are you clear on the criteria you are using to assess your employees? Are your employees clear on the criteria you are using to assess them?
3. How are you measuring your success as a manager?

References

Boswell, J. F., Kraus, D. R., Miller, S. D., & Lambert, M. J. (2015). Implementing routine outcome monitoring in clinical practice: Benefits, challenges, and solutions. *Psychotherapy Research, 25*(1), 6–19. https://doi.org/10.1080/10503307.2013.817696

Bracken, D., & Rose, D. (2011). When does 360-degree feedback create behavior change? And how would we know it when it does? *Journal of Business and Psychology, 26*(2), 183–192. https://doi.org/10.1007/s10869-011-9218-5

Gastaud, M. B., Feil, C. F., Merg, M. G., & Nunes, M. L. T. (2014). Psychological assessment as a protective factor against treatment dropout in psychoanalytic child psychotherapy of children: Empirical data. *Psicologia: Reflexão & Crítica, 27*(3), 498–503. https://doi.org/10.1590/1678-7153.201427310

Informing Change. (2017). *A guide to organizational capacity assessment tools: Finding—and using—the right tool for the job.* Retrieved January 24, 2020, from https://hewlett.org/wp-content/uploads/2017/11/A-Guide-to-Using-OCA-Tools.pdf

Karkoulian, S., Assaker, G., & Hallak, R. (2016). An empirical study of 360-degree feedback, organizational justice, and firm sustainability. *Journal of Business Research, 69*(5), 1862–1867. https://doi.org/10.1016/j.jbusres.2015.10.070

Kataoka, S. H., Podell, J. L., Zima, B. T., Best, K., Sidhu, S., & Jura, M. B. (2014). MAP as a model for practice-based learning and improvement in child psychiatry training. *Journal of Clinical Child & Adolescent Psychology*, *43*(2), 312–322. https://doi.org/10.1080/1537 4416.2013.848773

Kendall, D. L., & Salas, E. (2004). Measuring team performance: Review of current methods and consideration of future needs. In J. W. Ness (Ed.), *Advances in human performance and cognitive engineering research* (Vol. 5, pp. 307–326). Bingley: Emerald Publishing Limited.

Kirchner, G. L., Marshall, D., & Poyner, S. R. (2017). Mandated psychological assessments for suicide risk in a college population: A pilot study. *Journal of College Student Psychotherapy*, *31*(3), 192–202. https://doi.org/10.1080/87568225.2016.1268941.

Lambert, M. J. (2010). *Prevention of treatment failure: The use of measuring, monitoring, & feedback in clinical practice*. Washington, DC: American Psychological Association Press.

Lambert, M. J., & Harmon, K. L. (2018). The merits of implementing routine outcome monitoring in clinical practice. *Clinical Psychology: Science and Practice*, *25*(4), e12268. https://doi.org/10.1111/cpsp.12268

Northouse, P. G. (2013). *Leadership: Theory and practice*. Los Angeles, CA: SAGE.

Silver Wolf, D. A. P. (2018). The new social work. *Journal of Evidence-Informed Social Work*, *15*(6), 695–706. https://doi.org/10.1080/23761407.2018.1521321

Peralta, C. F., Lourenço, P. R., Lopes, P. N., Baptista, C., & Pais, L. (2018). Team development: Definition, measurement and relationships with team effectiveness. *Human Performance*, *31*(2), 97–124. https://doi.org/10.1080/08959285.2018.1455685

Tilsen, J., & McNamee, S. (2014). Feedback informed treatment: Evidence-based practice meets social construction. *Family Process*, *54*(1), 124–137. https://doi.org/10.1111/famp.12111

Tuckman, B., & Jensen, M. (1977). Stages of small-group development revisited. *Group & Organization Studies*, *2*(4), 419–427. https://doi.org/10.1177/105960117700200404

Youngman, J. (2017). The use and abuse of pre-employment personality tests. *Business Horizons*, *60*(3), 261–269. https://doi.org/10.1016/j.bushor.2016.11.010

Part Three

Intervention

If everything goes smoothly, intervention is much like ongoing case management or care coordination for employees; supervisors and managers work with staff to set goals for productivity, quality, efficiency, and professional development and supervisors provide support, encouragement, and resources to help employees achieve these goals. However, working in social services is rarely smooth sailing and clinical strategies can be adapted to respond effectively to crises (Chapter 7), resistance to change (Chapter 8), and when employees and workgroups have performance problems (Chapter 9). Emphasis is placed on collaborating with employees to solve problems to improve individual, team, and organizational outcomes.

7 Crisis Management

Once Upon a Time

Several years ago, I was walking into the restroom at work when my cell phone began to ring. Without looking at my phone, I hit the button to send it to voicemail. Call me weird, but I do not like to talk on the phone when I am in the bathroom. When it rang again a minute later, I again sent it to voicemail. Then I heard the ding of an incoming text message, immediately followed by two more. I looked at my screen to see who was trying to reach me – two missed calls and three texts from my boss. I spent the entire morning putting out fires and I just wanted a few minutes of peace while I answered the call of nature. The texts said, "call me." I sighed because I knew what was next. A loud beep sounded followed by my boss calling my name over and over. My company-issued phone also functioned as a walkie-talkie. How convenient. I engaged the talk button, summoned my most patient voice, and said, "Yes?"

What was the big emergency? I cannot remember. This was a near daily occurrence. At this agency, everything was treated like a crisis that required everyone to drop whatever they were doing to respond. It was exhausting, to say the least. This organization operated in perpetual crisis mode. If there was not a "crisis of the day," it was because there were multiple "crises of the day."

While it is not possible to avoid crises altogether, continual crisis mode is not healthy. Over time, this state of routine crisis took a toll on workers and managers alike; staff turnover went up, productivity went down. The energy spent just getting through the day left no room for contemplation and planning. I began to notice that our perpetual crisis mirrored the lives of many of our clients. How could we help our clients gain control over their chaotic lives if we could not gain control over our chaotic work lives?

Thankfully, there were some changes in the organization that allowed us to move out of continual crisis mode. Better policies and procedures were put in place, along with staff training that gave people more control over the flow of their day. No one shed any tears when the walkie-talkie cell phones were phased out.

Overture

Unfortunately, the experience described previously is far too common. In the messy world of human service delivery, where our jobs often revolve around responding to other people's crises, we can get swept up in the chaos. And for many clients, the crises are very real. If you work in a hospital, you may see patients experiencing a severe health crisis; if you work for children's services, you may help children who have been severely abused and at risk of serious harm; and if you work in a program serving people with serious mental illness, you may conduct suicide and homicide assessments on a very regular basis. Even in workplaces where we traditionally expect crises to be less life threatening, counselors are being prepared to respond to increased levels of threat, such as violence and sexual assault on school and college campuses. The good news is that you are likely already well trained and relatively experienced at crisis intervention, and the approach you use with your clients is equally applicable as supervisors and managers. As with clients, your goal is to de-escalate and stabilize and then take steps to prevent future crises. Applying this same over-arching approach will help you and your team, and hopefully your organization, stay out of crisis mode and create a more stable and higher-functioning work environment.

The Micro Arena

In clinical practice, a client typically experiences a crisis when an event or cir-cumstance disrupts their emotional equilibrium, their usual coping skills have failed, and as a result, their day-to-day functioning is significantly impaired (Flannery & Everly, 2000). The crisis may be developmental, situational, existential, or ecosystemic (Miller, 2012). When the crisis is acute, emotional instability is typically accompanied by physical, cognitive, and social disturbance (Shulman, 2009). In response, the individual attempts to mobilize resources and supports (personal, family, social, and/or environmental) to return to homeo-stasis. It is during this time that individuals often feel vulnerable and tend to be open to intervention. This is the critical window that is often referred to when we talk about crisis as an opportunity for change. Successfully navigating a crisis has been shown to promote personal growth, increase self-efficacy, and enhance community connectedness (Hepworth, Rooney, Rooney, & Strom-Gottfried, 2013). Unfortunately, sometimes the crisis is resolved without such positive outcomes and the individual returns to the same or an even worse state.

In direct practice, crisis intervention helps the client stabilize, mitigates the potential impact, activates resources and supports, normalizes the experience, and establishes an acceptable level of functioning. The practitioner assesses the individual's reaction to the crisis, their perceived vulnerability, and their affec-tive and behavioral functioning in order to determine the best response and fashion the most effective interventions. The most common crisis intervention strategies are the six steps outlined by James (2008). The first three focus on listening: assessment and problem definition, exploring and establishing safety, and providing support. The next three are more action oriented: examining alternatives, making plans, and obtaining commitment.

As with any client-provider interaction, there are cultural factors to consider during crisis intervention. The individual or family culture can impact how they respond to a crisis, their help-seeking behavior, and the impact of environmental and contextual factors (Hepworth et al., 2013). Individual, family, and community characteristics and strengths can also be leveraged to support crisis resolution.

As with the initial story, sometimes the crisis is not a one-time occurrence; some clients live in a perpetual state of crisis and additional steps are needed. Anticipatory guidance can help prepare clients to more successfully navigate future crises. Identifying and responding to the underlying causes of recurrent crises is often required to prevent future crises.

Other factors that clinicians consider are the type of stress resulting from the crisis and the best counseling response. General and critical stress responses are relatively normal and can be easier to overcome, while cumulative and post-traumatic stress can have a significant impact on long-term functioning if not appropriately treated (Flannery & Everly, 2000). For some clients and situations, a non-directive or collaborative approach is sufficient and builds client self-efficacy. For others, the counselor must be directive, advising the client on what needs to be done to establish safety and potentially taking action themselves, such as calling law enforcement, contacting child or adult protective services, or initiating hospitalization.

Crises are often complex and difficult to resolve and the life experiences of the crisis counselor can greatly influence the effectiveness of their intervention efforts (James, 2008). For example, the provider's past and current exposure to trauma can impact their emotional equilibrium and coping capacity. As a human services provider, it is critical that you remain calm and provide a safe holding space for your client in crisis. When your client is overwhelmed with lower-level emotional activation, your own ability to mobilize higher-level executive functioning is needed if you are to assist them with effective problem-solving.

The Macro Arena

Crises in the workplace can vary significantly. At the extreme, you may have to respond to serious threats of harm to staff and clients, such as active shooter situations, fire, or natural disasters. Sometimes, the crisis can be staff-related due to an employee's personal issues or serious health issues. Other times, the crisis can be client-related, such as when a client is harmed or threatens harm while receiving services at your agency. Personnel issues, lost contracts, and financial mismanagement are some of the many crises that you may encounter as a supervisor or manager. Any one of these issues can disrupt the day-to-day functioning of the team, destabilizing team members emotionally, cognitively, physically,

58 *Intervention*

and socially. As with clients, a crisis can be an opportunity for positive change and increased team efficacy and connectedness, or it can derail your team and performance can take a nosedive that lasts long after the crisis is resolved. In large part, you can play a significant role in the outcome for your team.

Whatever the crisis, as a supervisor or manager you need to remain calm and apply appropriate intervention strategies. Your job is to stabilize the situation, mitigate the impact, activate resources, normalize responses to the crisis, and, as quickly as possible, restore an acceptable level of functioning in the workplace. The challenge is that you are not just assessing one individual to determine the level and type of intervention needed, but rather several individuals all at once. The upside is that you will likely have one or two team members who cope with crisis very well and can support and bolster those who do not. They will become key resources you can mobilize and deploy to serve as your proxy depending on the situation. If the crisis is amenable to a group intervention and the team was high functioning prior to the crisis, this can be an especially effective approach as team members provide mutual support and the team leader can be less directive. However, sometimes the crisis is confidential in nature (e.g., personnel issue) or is best handled with only those directly affected.

The same six steps described previously work particularly well in the macro environment. However, if you have a different procedure for crisis intervention with clients at your agency, it will invariably align with the steps you need to take as a leader. You will want to make a quick and thorough assessment of the situation, be clear about the problem, establish safety for both staff and the general public, and provide support to your team and the larger community if affected. The action phase may need to happen very quickly depending on the level of threat, or you may be able to take your time to deliberate on the alternatives and weigh out the pros and cons. If the threat is high, you will want to involve managers or supervisors to help identify the best response and support your decision. You will also want to involve your team members in developing a mitigation plan. As with clients, involving your staff in plan development is crucial to get buy-in and follow through. All too often, it is this last piece that is often forgotten as leadership becomes involved and takes over – sometimes due to their own panic response – and then dictates the solution without engaging employees in this important part of the crisis resolution process.

Individual and team culture can also affect crisis response in the workplace and expectations of your role in the crisis response as the supervisor. If some team members, or perhaps the entire team, are highly deferential to those in a position of authority, they may look to you to be directive and take charge. On the other hand, an independent team may resent you for stepping in and telling them what to do even if you feel the situation warrants that you be directive in terms of who should do what and when. If the crisis is for the entire organization and your team is affected by it, you may find that your superiors are telling you exactly what to do. Like with the opening story, you may have little choice but to jump and respond to a crisis-addicted leader. Your challenge is to protect your staff from having the same experience as you by engaging them collaboratively in all phases of the crisis response.

Your relationship with your team pre-crisis will influence the crisis response. Employees who have a positive relationship with you are less likely to place blame on you or the organization. What you have done as a supervisor or manager to foster a positive relationship may be more important than any crisis intervention strategy that you employ (Brown & White, 2010). Leaders who establish positive interpersonal relationships with their employees can more easily motivate and engage them to participate in crisis intervention activities to successfully navigate change (Graham, Robbins, McGivern, & Spangenburg, 2008).

Risk management as an administrator will likely be experienced differently than as a direct service provider. Your role is not only to ensure a client or staff member is safe, but also to manage communication with the public or other key stakeholders. Part of crisis resolution is to manage the communication both inside and outside of the organization. This entails consistent messaging from leadership, being attentive to informal staff communication regarding the crisis, and keeping an eye out for news stories and social media posts. As a supervisor, you may not be required to respond to media inquiries, but you will need to provide key facts and critical information to those that do. You may also need to guide team members on how to react to questions from the public or media. As with your staff, your pre-crisis relationship and communication with the community and key stakeholders will help facilitate a more positive post-crisis response (Sellnow, 2015). While it may feel unseemly to have to "sell" a story to the public, when thought of as "renewal discourse," effective post-crisis communication has been shown to help large organizations recover from horrific losses and can serve as a renewing force to help a devastated workforce reframe a crisis and find a way forward (Seeger, Ulmer, Novak, & Sellnow, 2005).

This Is How We Do It

As a manager, crisis situations present you with a variety of threats. Three ways to classify these threats are as follows: safety, financial, and reputational. First, safety threats include physical and psychological harm. Second, financial threats include monetary loss and liability. Lastly, reputational threats include loss of esteem and bad publicity. These threats can be inter-related; for example, a senior manager who embezzles from the organization (financial threat) can result in damaged public trust in the organization (reputational threat). Another example is that a young client harming himself (safety threat) can turn into a financial threat if the client's family sues the organization for improper care (financial threat). If the client's family speaks to a reporter and it winds up on the news, the organization could also lose its standing in the community (reputational threat).

The first step in crisis intervention is usually some type of safety assessment. It is important that you deal with threats in the correct order – safety threats must be dealt with first. Your primary concern must be individual and public safety. Other threats should only be considered after safety threats have been addressed.

The following table goes into more detail about each type of threat, as well as providing examples and assessment questions you can ask.

60 *Intervention*

Table 7.1

Type of Threat	Examples	Possible Assessment Questions
Safety	• Physical harm • Psychological harm • Present or imminent harm	• Has anyone been injured? • Is anyone in physical danger? • Is anyone in psychological distress? • Do we need to perform a suicidality assessment? • Do we need to contact law enforcement or emergency medical or psychiatric services? • What aspects of this could lead to financial or reputational threats?
Financial	• Embezzlement • Property loss or damage • Loss of funding	• Is there damage to or loss of company property? • Are there any security breaches to the organization's data networks or databases? • Has money been stolen or misappropriated? • What aspects of this could lead to safety or reputational threats?
Reputational	• Bad publicity • Loss of public trust	• What is known or believed about this incident internally? What is known or believed externally? • What, if anything, needs to be communicated internally? Externally? • What aspects of this need to be kept confidential (due to client rights, Health Insurance Portability and Accountability Act (HIPAA), etc.)? • What aspects of this could lead to safety or financial threats?

Case Study

June supervised ten school social workers, each of whom were assigned to a different site in a small school district. Sofia was her newest school counselor, having graduated from a master's program just five months earlier. One early Monday morning, Sofia called June to report that a teacher committed suicide over the weekend. The school principal and district superintendent were going to gather faculty and staff before school to break the news and they wanted Sofia to help counsel the teachers. Sofia sounded in a panic as she conveyed this to June between sobs and gasping breaths. June asked Sofia to take some deep breaths with her to help calm and center herself. She told Sofia that she would head to the school but would not arrive before the school bell, so Sofia would need to meet with the teachers without her. To help prepare Sofia, June took a directive approach by reminding Sofia of the crisis intervention steps and encouraging her to listen, reflect, empathize, and engage with the faculty and staff. Then, she asked Sofia what else she needed. Sofia said she was concerned that the school and district did not have protocols in place for this type of situation and that she felt overwhelmed at the prospect of being the only counselor on site at the school. June said she would meet with the principal and superintendent when she arrived at the school. She also said she would notify the district's other school counselors and make sure they were ready to head to the school. In addition, she would contact a local counseling agency to mobilize them for on-site counseling. While June drove to the school, Sofia met with faculty and staff, where they processed what happened and came up with a plan to get through the school day.

When June arrived, she met with the principal and superintendent and provided education on how to manage grief and loss on the campus and mitigate possible suicide contagion as well as crafting communication to the parents, community, and media. School social workers from the district helped by going to each of the classrooms and supporting the teachers and students. Therapists from the counseling agency June contacted met with students individually and in small groups.

Sofia focused on working with the deceased teacher's class, especially those students who experienced the greatest shock. She sat and listened as they grieved and asked them how they wanted to memorialize their teacher. They chose to create an art project on one of the classroom walls and invited the rest of the school to contribute. In the days and weeks ahead, another group of students approached Sofia and asked if they could do a suicide prevention campaign for the school. Sofia established an ongoing grief group for students focused on their own losses rather than the teacher's death.

The follow up would continue, but in a very short period of time, June provided crisis intervention to her staff member and guided her on how to do the same with the teachers. She remained calm and quickly helped to stabilize Sofia through deep breathing and reassurance. In addition, she made a brief assessment of the situation and identified the resources she would mobilize to bring to the scene. Determining that Sofia needed direction, June took a directive approach so that Sofia knew exactly what to do. She then engaged Sofia in some planning by asking her what she needed. She mobilized community resources to support the students and teachers. Lastly, she worked with administration to develop communication plans and protocols for handling crises in the future.

Key Takeaways

- During a crisis, your job is to identify and mitigate the threats, facilitate recovery, and gets things back to normal.
- A crisis brings three types of threats that are often inter-related: safety, financial, and reputational.
- Safety threats should be dealt with first.
- Communication (internal and external) during and after the crisis is essential (as is realizing you are not the only one communicating at these times).

Discussion Questions

1. Does your organization have a crisis-management plan?
2. If so, is your staff aware of the plan?
3. Does your plan prioritize threats to safety?

References

Brown, K., & White, C. (2010). Organization–public relationships and crisis response strategies: Impact on attribution of responsibility. *Journal of Public Relations Research, 23*(1), 75–92. https://doi.org/10.1080/1062726X.2010.504792

Flannery, R. B., & Everly, G. S. (2000). Crisis intervention: A review. *International Journal of Emergency Mental Health, 2*(2), 119–126.

Graham, J., Robbins, S., McGivern, M., & Spangenburg, J. (2008). *Leadership and change in a crisis organization: An exploratory analysis of the relationship between leadership style and employee perception* (Publication No. 3339019). ProQuest Dissertations Publishing.

Hepworth, D. H., Rooney, R. H., Rooney, D. G., & Strom-Gottfried, K. (2013). *Direct social work practice: Theory and skills.* Belmont, CA: Brooks/Cole.

James, R. K. (2008). *Crisis intervention strategies.* Belmont, CA: Thomson Brooks/Cole.

Miller, G. (2012). *Fundamentals of crisis counseling.* Hoboken, NJ: Wiley and Sons.

Shulman, L. (2009). *The skills of helping individuals, families, groups, and communities* (6th ed.). Belmont, CA: Brooks/Cole.

Seeger, M., Ulmer, R., Novak, J., & Sellnow, T. (2005). Post-crisis discourse and organizational change, failure and renewal. *Journal of Organizational Change Management, 18*(1), 78–95. https://doi.org/10.1108/09534810510579869

Sellnow, T. L. (2015). *The SAGE handbook of risk communication.* Thousand Oaks, CA: SAGE.

8 Resistance to Change

Once Upon a Time

A few months after I took over as a program manager at a non-profit organization, I learned that I was required to complete an annual report. As I began to gather information, I discovered that most of the case managers had not been completing the intake paperwork or data entry since the program began a year earlier. I met with the case managers and they told me that they had not been doing it consistently because the intake form was too long. When I asked about data entry, Martha, the most senior of the staff, rolled her eyes and said, "Like we have time for that!" Her peers nodded in agreement and clearly felt the conversation was over. Panicked that we would be out of compliance, I told them firmly that this would need to change. I clearly instructed them to use the long-form intake (they had developed a shorthand written form for internal use) and to begin to enter data immediately. I followed up with a written memo. One week later, not one of the case managers had entered any data, five of the seven new intakes submitted to me were still on the short form, and the two long forms were incomplete.

I decided to meet with staff individually to understand the workflow and barriers to completing this required task. I met with Martha for our regularly scheduled supervision and brought up the topic. She told me this was an impossible request of her and her colleagues. I expounded on the reasons why we needed to do the tasks and the potential ramifications of failing to do state-mandated paperwork and data entry. I explained that the data entry was being used for a larger research project and our failure to do this so far had compromised the study. I tried to make the case that both tasks were important, but she came back by saying, "If we really want to help families, we can't be spending our time doing paperwork." It seemed the more I argued for my position, the more she argued back and things began to feel tense. As a fairly new manager, I was wary about creating such conflict with one of my key staff, but I also had to change their behavior. Completing documentation in a timely fashion was non-negotiable. I recall stating somewhat tersely, "If you don't do the paperwork, this program won't get funded and then you can't help any families because you won't have a job!" We glared at each other and dug in our heels. We were at a standstill and I would need to find another approach.

64 *Intervention*

Overture

Whether you are a direct practitioner or an administrator, your primary charge is to facilitate change. Working with clients, your focus is usually on behavior change. People seeking counseling or social services typically want to change their life circumstances, whether it is to find employment, relieve physical or mental health symptoms, or reduce negative and enhance positive behaviors to improve quality of life. Supervisors and managers are inevitably in the same business, as their role is to decrease negative workplace behaviors and increase positive behaviors in order to help employees meet the needs of the clients seeking change. If you supervise or manage a professional workforce, your employees will often view you as someone who is there to help them grow and develop professionally and they actively seek and embrace change. However, sometimes the employee, like the client, does not recognize the need to change and is interacting with you because someone else has identified the need to change or their behavior has created a significant problem for them or others. In these situations, you will find several strategies used when working with clients that translate quite effectively to the personnel management arena.

The other challenge in the workplace is employee resistance to organizational changes. Sometimes, these changes are out of your control, such as the introduction of a new policy, implementation of a new tool, or agency reorganization. Other times, the change is something you have identified as necessary to improve workflow or teamwork. As a supervisor or manager, it is your responsibility to identify and lead change to correct problems in your workgroup related to low productivity, poor work quality, or a failure to achieve the organizational goals assigned to your workgroup. While the change may look quite different as a supervisor or manager, the dynamics of change, resistance to change, and the techniques employed to help individuals navigate change are surprisingly similar. We contend that if you consciously apply the theories and practices you know about change from your work with clients to your work with your employees, you will have a strong advantage over your peers when it comes to leading change in the workplace.

The Micro Arena

When we begin to work in the helping profession, we often resort to giving advice. Many of us get into this profession because we are good problem solvers and have clarity about other people's problems that they seem to lack. When we see people struggling with life challenges and failing, our righting reflex kicks in and we want to fix the situation. It can come as a surprise when our advice is not acted upon or even welcomed. Our efforts to help often include preaching, lecturing, teaching, directing, or even confronting. Sadly, these approaches can breed resentment, increase resistance, and often result in retreat. Over time, with training and experience, we learn that through listening, empathy, and gentle evocative questioning, our clients feel more affirmed and accepted and are more likely to embrace change. It is unfortunate that we often have to relearn this lesson as supervisors and managers.

Ambivalence to change and readiness for change in direct practice with clients has attracted a lot of attention. MI, developed over 30 years ago by Dr. William Miller and Dr. Stephen Rollnick, is arguably the best known and most well-researched method of helping clients resolve their ambivalence when it comes to changing behavior. Emerging from the field of addictions, resistance and motivation are viewed in an interpersonal context, where a collaborative conversational style is employed to strengthen a client's motivation and commitment to change.

Ambivalence is a normal state that affects many areas of one's life. People become stuck when they have conflicting feelings about a situation (Miller & Rollnick, 2012). To facilitate change, people need to believe they can change and that their counselors believe in them. People arrive at this belief when given the opportunity to talk about change in a safe, non-judgmental, and caring space. Intrinsic motivation to change emerges in the context of accepting and empowering relationships where the painful present can be acknowledged. Extrinsic motivation can be generated through fear and reward, but such motivation is short lived. It is long-lasting, intrinsic motivation that the counselor wants to elicit in order to help clients embrace healthier behaviors.

If you are not familiar with MI, we strongly urge you to attend a training, watch a webinar, or purchase a workbook to learn more about this very powerful set of counseling techniques. Briefly, there are several acronyms in MI to retain the key principles and skills. For example, you can **d**evelop discrepancy, **e**xpress empathy, **a**mplify ambivalence, **r**oll with resistance, and **s**upport self-efficacy (DEARS). Key skills include **a**ffirmations, **r**eflective listening, **o**pen-ended questions, **s**ummarization, and **e**liciting change talk (AROSE). MI engages four fundamental processes: establishing a partnership (engage), clarifying their agenda (focus), eliciting reasons for change (evoke), and committing to a plan of action (plan).

MI has demonstrated efficacy in addressing a wide range of behavioral issues (Copeland, McNamara, Kelson, & Simpson, 2015), including medication adherence, anxiety disorders (Marker & Norton, 2018), oral health in adolescents (Wu et al., 2017), HIV management (Dillard, Zuniga, & Holstad, 2017), alcohol and drug use (D'Amico et al., 2018), and more. It has more recently been applied in the macro arena (Hohman, 2012; Wilcox, Kersh, & Jenkins, 2017), and Dr. William Miller has expressed an interest in studying MI in supervision, management, and leadership (W. Miller, personal communication, April 17, 2017).

The Macro Arena

As a supervisor, manager, administrator, or leader in the human services industry, a key challenge is to help your organization be adaptable in the face of societal changes. This means guiding your employees to adapt to the requirements of organizational changes. However, change initiatives often fail and employee resistance is frequently cited as the primary cause (Wittig, 2012). Organizational changes will typically require behavior changes and some employees will feel ambivalent about changing their behavior. Humans are hardwired to prefer their own ideas over those produced by others (Feldstein Ewing, Yezhuvath, Houck, & Filbey, 2014), and yet organizational changes are usually top-down.

66 *Intervention*

A key challenge is to help your staff resolve their ambivalence and empower them to embrace the role they can have in influencing the change process.

In their New York Times bestselling book *Switch: How to Change Things When Change Is Hard*, Heath and Heath (2010) described the role of emotions and rationality when it comes to change by conjuring up the image of the elephant and the rider. The elephant represents the emotions while the rider is rationality; the authors argued that while we may assume the rider controls the elephant, it is often the other way around. Ideally, the rider and the elephant are working together to get where they need to go, but sadly the relationship is generally more like a battle. Your staff may know that the new policy, procedure, or process will make work more efficient or productive, but the effort required to learn a new task or adapt to a new team structure feels overwhelming and the status quo offers comfort and familiarity. The elephant is large and can refuse to move.

The first step is to engage your employee in a conversation about change and this needs to involve a recognition of the emotional investment in not changing. If you appeal only to the rational side of the argument, providing a list of reasons why the change is needed, the elephant is left out of the equation and remains seated and immobile. It is only once you address how your employee feels about the change, acknowledge the discomfort, and understand why the change feels difficult that both elephant and rider (feelings and thoughts) can fully engage in participatory decision-making. Our experience is that MI techniques will serve you well as you work through this process with your staff, and that investing the time up front will increase the number of early adopters and prevent sabotage.

Some may argue that using techniques originally designed for clinical intervention with clinicians themselves will not work because they will know what you are doing and will "see through" your strategy as an attempt to make them change. If this were the case, then therapists, counselors, and clinicians would never go to therapy or counseling since they know all of the techniques being used on them as a client. If you have ever sought counseling yourself, you know this is far from the truth, and that usually the opposite is true. Not only do you experience the positive effects of the intervention, but you also get to observe someone putting the techniques into action, providing a role model of sorts. Even if you have not sought counseling yourself (which we strongly encourage you to do whether or not you are or have ever been a clinician), role playing MI with a peer will show you that even if it feels awkward as the interviewer to use prescribed techniques, the application of reflecting, summarizing, affirmations, and open-ended questions feels good as the interviewee. This is not therapy, but rather a good way to be a caring and compassionate human being who interacts with the intent to understand people better and help them find the intrinsic motivation to make needed change.

This Is How We Do It

Let's walk through the use of MI in a clinical application as compared to a management application. You will see that the application bears many similarities, with the key difference being the management application keeps the focus on work.

Resistance to Change   67

Table 8.1

Stage and Purpose	Clinical Application	Management Application
Engaging: establishing a partnership	• What's been going on with you since our last session? • What are some of the things that have been going well for you?	• What's been going on with you since our last meeting? • What are some of the things that have been going well for you at work?
Focusing: clarifying their agenda	• What would you like to focus on for our session today? • What are your concerns? • What would you like to change about your current situation?	• What would you like to focus on for our meeting today? • What are your concerns today? • If you were to change something about (your area of concern), what would that be?
Evoking: eliciting reasons for change	• How important is this to you on a scale of zero to ten? • Why is this important to you? • What helps you know that you could do this?	• How important is this to you on a scale of zero to ten? • Why is this important to you? • How can I support you in this?
Planning: committing to a plan of action	• What do you want the end outcome to be? • How do you see this happening? • What are your first steps?	• What do you want the end outcome to be? • What will you do to make this happen? • What are your first steps?

Case Study

Helping Hands Inc. received a new grant to help parolees find stable employment and housing. Joe was asked to implement this new program in addition to the veteran housing program where he currently supervised case managers. Joe, a Navy veteran, had an undergraduate degree in criminal justice and had worked with several veterans who had been in jail at one point or another, so he embraced the challenge. To begin implementation immediately, however, he would need to bring two of his current case managers over to the new program while he went about recruiting and hiring additional staff. There were two case managers he believed would be an asset to the program, and while the first jumped at the opportunity, the second, Luke, stated that he would prefer that Joe ask someone else.

Joe told Luke he had asked him because he really appreciated his work ethic, creativity, and ability to engage resistant clients (*affirmation*) and

68   *Intervention*

these were all skills Joe really needed to be successful in implementing this new program. Luke responded that he appreciated the recognition and wanted to help, but he liked what he was currently doing. Joe said, "you would like to be a team player and help out, but you really like where you're at" (*reflection*). "Exactly!" Luke replied. Joe asked Luke to tell him what the downside would be in changing positions (*evocative question*) and Luke talked about having to transition current clients to another worker and the impact it would have, especially for one or two clients who were close to securing permanent housing. He talked about the stress of learning a new program and his fear that he would not understand the needs of parolees the way he did the veterans (Luke was also a veteran). Joe *reflected* and *summarized* Luke's responses. He then asked about the upside of taking on this new role (*evocative question*). Luke spoke about how he would enjoy learning something new, that it would expand his repertoire, and that he believed in the mission of the agency. Once again, Joe *reflected* and *summarized* his responses.

Joe asked Luke where he saw himself in three to five years (*evocative question*); Luke said that he wanted to be a supervisor like Joe. Joe asked him to tell him more about this. Luke said he admired the way that Joe led and coached his team to make a real difference in the community. Joe told Luke he could certainly see him in that role and believed he had the potential to be an excellent supervisor and even a manager one day (*affirmation, hope*). Joe then asked what Luke thought he would need to do to become a supervisor (*open-ended question*). Luke said he would need to continue to learn more about the agency and the populations they serve and take some training in supervision. He also said he thought he needed an additional one to two years working with clients directly to really learn all aspects of case management and community resource development. Joe reflected, "In addition to training, in order to be ready to be a supervisor, you want to increase your experience and get to know the agency and community better." Luke confirmed this and then said, "I guess learning a new program would be a good first step then?" and smiled, realizing that Joe had led him right to where Joe wanted him. "But, what about my clients? They've been through so much and they trust me, especially Len and Marv. I don't want to abandon them." Joe *reflected*, "You are worried that some of your clients will regress if you leave them. It's your dedication to your clients that I so appreciate and part of the reason I was hoping you could come to the new program. But I see your challenge."

Having had a discussion about both thoughts and feelings, Joe decided to move into participatory decision-making. He already had a possible solution but wanted Luke to find a way forward rather than impose it on him. Joe said, "It seems that while you have an interest in taking me up on this offer, your commitment to your clients keeps you where you are. Do you see anyway to work around this?" Luke thought for a while and said, "Could I transition slowly? Maybe transfer some of the newer cases and close the cases that are pretty stable, but keep my higher risk cases for the time being?" Joe agreed this was a good idea and suggested Luke review his caseload and come back tomorrow so they could determine which cases to transfer or close. Before he left, Luke thanked Joe for believing in him and helping him to find a way to move forward in his career while still doing right by his clients.

Key Takeaways

- When employees resist change, they are likely ambivalent about the change.
- By incorporating MI skills in your supervisory meetings, you provide employees with an opportunity to talk about their ambivalence to change.
- MI for management promotes employee engagement and facilitates employee buy-in for organizational and team member goals.
- Core MI skills that you can use with your team are open-ended questions, affirmations, reflective listening, and summarizing.

Discussion Questions

1. Do your employees only perform due to fear of disciplinary action and monetary incentives or are they creative, responsible, and hardworking? How might your beliefs about your employees shape your management style?
2. How much of your supervision time with direct reports is spent telling them what to do versus asking questions and carefully listening?
3. What can you do to build a culture of partnership, mutual trust, and respect with your team?

References

Copeland, L., McNamara, R., Kelson, M., & Simpson, S. (2015). Mechanisms of change within motivational interviewing in relation to health behaviors outcomes: A systematic review. *Patient Education and Counseling, 98*(4), 401–411. https://doi.org/10.1016/j. pec.2014.11.022

D'Amico, E. J., Parast, L., Shadel, W. G., Meredith, L. S., Seelam, R., & Stein, B. D. (2018). Brief motivational interviewing intervention to reduce alcohol and marijuana use for at-risk adolescents in primary care. *Journal of Consulting and Clinical Psychology, 86*(9), 775–786. https://doi.org/10.1037/ccp0000332

Dillard, P. K., Zuniga, J. A., & Holstad, M. M. (2017). An integrative review of the efficacy of motivational interviewing in HIV management. *Patient Education and Counseling, 100*(4), 636–646. https://doi.org/10.1016/j.pec.2016.10.029

70 Intervention

Feldstein Ewing, S. W., Yezhuvath, U., Houck, J. M., & Filbey, F. M. (2014). Brain-based origins of change language: A beginning. *Addictive Behaviors, 39*(12), 1904–1910. https://doi.org/10.1016/j.addbeh.2014.07.035

Heath, C., & Heath, D. (2010). *Switch: How to change things when change is hard.* New York: Random House.

Hohman, M. (2012). *Motivational interviewing in social work practice.* New York: Guilford Press.

Marker, I., & Norton, P. J. (2018). The efficacy of incorporating motivational interviewing to cognitive behavior therapy for anxiety disorders: A review and meta-analysis. *Clinical Psychology Review, 62,* 1–10. https://doi.org/10.1016/j.cpr.2018.04.004

Miller, W. R., & Rollnick, S. (2012). *Motivational interviewing: Helping people change.* New York: Guilford Press.

Wilcox, J., Kersh, B. C., & Jenkins, E. A. (2017). *Motivational interviewing for leadership: MI-LEAD.* Roseburg, OR: Gray Beach Publishing.

Wittig, C. (2012). Employees' reactions to organizational change. *OD Practitioner, 44*(2), 23–28.

Wu, L., Gao, X., Lo, E. C. M., Ho, S. M. Y., McGrath, C., & Wong, M. C. M. (2017). Motivational interviewing to promote oral health in adolescents. *Journal of Adolescent Health, 61*(3), 378–384. https://doi.org/10.1016/j.jadohealth.2017.03.010

9 Performance Issues

Once Upon a Time

As a program manager for a non-profit organization that provided community-based programs for children and families, I finished up a weekly staff meeting with the "other business" part of the agenda. I asked if anyone had any other business and Mark, who ran the after-school program, raised his hand. Mark said he wanted to revisit the issue of how referrals were processed in the department. Several people rolled their eyes and a few audibly sighed. Mark ignored them and launched into his issue. Once again, Mark described in detail how long it took for families of the kids at the after-school program to get counseling and other supportive services through the agency. He complained that the delay was jeopardizing his program's contract requirements. The supervisors from the other programs were less concerned about the delay because their programs were already exceeding their numbers. They suggested, as they did every time this topic was discussed, that Mark refer the families out for services. Mark said other providers were similarly overwhelmed and that it should be easier to make in-house referrals. We talked about the issue, discussed various reasons for the problem, brainstormed possible solutions, shot down each of those solutions, and ran out of time. I promised we would return to the topic next week as the staff filed out of the room. This happened every week – rinse and repeat. As Mark and I sat in the now empty conference room, I wondered aloud if we would ever stop talking about this issue. Mark said if he was a client with an ongoing problem, the counselors would have figured out a way to help him solve it by now. I could not disagree and wondered whether there was a better way to solve this problem.

Overture

Performance problems for supervisors and managers are your macro equivalent to the client problems that bring people to your office every day as a direct practitioner. For your client, their problems have become so overwhelming that they either elect to seek help or have been directed to do so by another entity (e.g., parent, doctor, or judge). Similarly, your employee is proactively seeking

72   *Intervention*

your assistance with a client or workplace problem or has been directed to meet with you because their actions or inactions are negatively impacting individual, team, or organizational performance. This is a time when you can reach into your tool bag and pull from any number of clinical techniques to help your staff navigate these challenging times.

This is also a time to be especially mindful that your employee is not your client. It is an unfortunate error when the new supervisor relegates their well-honed interpersonal skills from the realm of therapy and counseling and in their place adopts a new persona as a "boss" who now talks instead of listens, directs instead of facilitates, and threatens instead of encourages. But it is just as treacherous to become the office therapist and forget your role as manager and leader. You need to live in that grey area of sharing responsibility while having the ultimate responsibility for outcomes; leading and yet following; being in control but not being controlling; steering the course while letting others take the wheel; being generous with praise while also holding folks accountable; sharing the big picture and keeping a close eye on the details; and, at the end of the day, always attributing success to your team and not to yourself. Look at this list again and think about how this is similar and different to working with clients. Depending on your role as a practitioner, it will give you an idea of how your skills with clients can be leveraged in your new role as a supervisor or manager.

The Micro Arena

There are multiple evidence-based practices in the clinical realm that hold great promise for application in the macro environment. In Chapter 7, we described MI as a way to address employee resistance to organizational change; in this chapter, we will discuss how to adapt two well-researched therapeutic interventions proven to be effective with different client groups in various settings and with diverse presenting problems in the human services arena. The first is Problem Solving Therapy (PST) and the second is Solution Focused Brief Therapy (SFBT). Even if you were not a clinician prior to being a supervisor or you did not use these particular interventions, you may find many of their components familiar and they are likely parts of other treatment approaches or intervention models used at your agency.

PST originated in the late 1960s as an offshoot of Cognitive Behavioral Therapy (CBT). Thomas D'Zurilla and Arthur Nezu developed the clinical application of the problem-solving process over the next few decades, resulting in a therapeutic intervention that includes defining the problem, generating alternative solutions, and doing effective decision-making (D'Zurilla, Nezu, & Maydeu-Olivares, 2004; Nezu & D'Zurilla, 2007). Research has subsequently demonstrated the effectiveness of this clinical intervention with people suffering from anxiety and depression and coping with various medical illnesses (Felgoise & Corvi, 2017). Replacing maladaptive problem-solving with adaptive problem-solving increases motivation, confidence, and productivity. It has been modified for various client populations and in various settings (e.g., groups and on-line), and is often used as an adjunctive to other therapies.

Problems addressed by PST can be personal, relational, or environmental, and can range from severe and chronic problems to normal problems of everyday life. Individuals are thought to have a problem-solving orientation that is either positive (rational), negative (impulsive), or avoidant, with the latter two causing significant distress. The goal of PST is to enhance a positive problem orientation and decrease a negative problem orientation in order to decrease stress and improve quality of life. PST begins with problem definition and clarification, followed by the generation of possible solutions through brainstorming. The next step is decision-making, which includes weighing the pros and cons and selecting an option. The final steps are developing an implementation plan and monitoring and evaluating the outcome. Various cognitive and behavioral techniques are employed to support problem-solving efforts such as challenging cognitive distortions and role playing. An effective solution is one that provides a satisfactory outcome for everyone involved (Eskin, 2013).

SFBT was developed in the early 1980s by Steve de Shazer and Insoo Kim Berg as an alternative to deficit-oriented therapy. The premise of this approach is that people know what they need to do to improve their own lives and are capable of finding the best solutions with appropriate coaching and questioning. Research on SFBT has found it to be effective with individuals, couples, and families; and it is beneficial with different cultures, backgrounds, and age groups. Based on a review of controlled-outcome studies of SFBT, Gingerich and Peterson (2013) found it to be effective for a wide range of behavioral and psychological issues and noted it was briefer than most alternate therapies and thus was far more cost-effective.

SFBT principles include looking for solutions in the present rather than focusing on the past, creating a collaborative partnership between clinician and client, and believing that small changes can lead to big results. Several SFBT techniques are likely familiar to you. Finding the exception asks the client to think about times when the problem was absent or lacked its usual potency, exploring how the exception is different from the usual experiences with the problem, and formulating a solution based on what sets the exception scenario apart. Another SFBT question relates to effective coping strategies already known or used by the client that can be applied to the problem at hand. This helps clients recognize their skills in coping with adversity, demonstrate their self-efficacy, and highlights their resiliency. Probably one of the most well-known questions in SFBT is the miracle question, when the client is asked to envision a future in which the problem does not exist and explain how their life would look different. Once they have this picture in their mind, they are asked to identify small, practical steps they can take immediately toward that change. Like MI and PST, SFBT often employs scaling questions to help clients assess the seriousness of the present circumstances and progress toward their goals to gain insight, to create hope, and to stimulate change.

SFBT increases motivation and produces positive behavior change. PST teaches practical skills to help clients not only solve a current problem, but also learn a process that can be applied in the future without the therapist's assistance. Both approaches focus on the present and on finding a quick solution to an immediate problem. Neither intervention is complex, and both have

74 *Intervention*

the flexibility to be used in conjunction with other approaches, making them especially amenable to the workplace environment.

The Macro Arena

Health and human service organizations often struggle to keep their workers engaged, motivated, and productive. This can be further complicated when supervisors and managers oversee an inter-professional workforce comprised of staff with different professional values and practice agendas. Supervisors and managers often inherit staff and teams with known performance issues. The pressure is on for the new supervisor or manager to solve problems quickly and demonstrate that they have the organizational and leadership skills to make dramatic improvements. The human services supervisor or manager facing these simultaneous challenges needs a toolkit of possible interventions to solve problems, improve performance, and enhance employee engagement. You already have several at your disposal, e.g., PST and SFBT, that align closely with those espoused in the supervisory, management, and leadership literature.

A number of management approaches mirror elements of PST and SFBT. There are many books that explore ways that managers can walk through the problem-solving process in organizations, similar to the process in PST (e.g., Carnarius, 1976; Kreitner, 1980; Ziegenfuss, 2002). Similarly, books or articles aiming to guide supervisors on effective supervision, performance management, and dealing with change inevitably include a section outlining a multi-step problem-solving method as described previously (e.g., Conlow, 2001; Roseman, 1985).

SF supervision, coaching, management, and leadership have been espoused by Godat (2006, 2013) as a powerful and practical way to achieve positive change with people, teams, and organizations. The author described SF interventions as ranging from short daily interactions to more extensive cyclical management processes. The actual techniques mirror those of SFBT with slightly different labels such as "Platform Building," "Discovering What Works," "Affirming," "Small Steps," and "Future Perfect" (Godat, 2013, p. 22). These collaborative activities between employees and managers or between stakeholders and leaders aim to quickly achieve desired outcomes.

SF management as an approach helps managers identify what is already working and amplifies it, focus on what is possible rather than on causes of problems, and stop doing what is not working and instead do something different. Possibilities are explored in the past, present, and future; small changes are used to achieve desired goals, and expertise for achieving solutions is located within the person or team wanting to change or improve (Cauffman, 2006).

Other management approaches that align with PST and SFBT are Management by Objectives (MBO), Strengths-Based Management, and Appreciative Inquiry (AI). Like SFBT, MBO empowers and motivates employees to set their own objectives, develop their skills, and provides reinforcement for progress toward their goals (Netting, Kettner, & McMurtry, 1993). Like SFBT, Strengths-Based Management focuses on competencies over weaknesses and empowering over managing, improving staff engagement, creativity, and productivity (Rath & Conchie, 2008).

Like PST, AI has defined steps starting with "discovery" when the problem is clarified; "dreaming," which is akin to the miracle question in SFBT; and then two final steps of "design" and "deliver," encompassing PST's approach to decision-making, plan implementation, and outcome evaluation (Cooperrider & Whitney, 2001).

You can probably see that you do not need to embark on developing an entirely new set of supervisory and management skills to jump into the arena of personnel management, performance improvement, or organizational change management. While delving into the books cited previously, reading up on these macro interventions, and attending related trainings will serve you well, you already have the most important elements of these approaches at your disposal. We encourage you to consider other interventions you have used effectively in direct practice, break them down into their component parts, and select those that seem applicable to the problem at hand. For example, a classic intervention commonly used in direct practice is behavioral rehearsal or role playing. When a client is anxious about trying a new behavior such as a conversation with a boss, spouse, or child, you would likely suggest they practice with you first in the safety of the counseling office. This same approach is particularly helpful for supervisees who can rehearse an anticipated interaction with a client or co-worker in the safety and privacy of the supervisor's office. Do not abandon the tools you already have that are generally useful when helping people enhance behavioral functioning; review what you know, repackage and relabel, and then reapply as appropriate in your new context as supervisor, manager, or leader.

This Is How We Do It

Applying SFBT to supervision and management involves four key steps detailed in the following table:

Table 9.1

Step	Questions	Purpose
Acknowledge Problems	• What is the essence of the problem? • How does it impact you?	Identify the problem but don't get bogged down on the causes
Describe Success	• What would it look like if the problem went away? • How will you know if success happens?	Create a picture of what you're trying to achieve
Identify Exceptions	• When have things worked well in the past? • What was different then?	Find times when the problem lacked its usual potency
Take a Small Step Forward	• Which part(s) of step 3 could you do again? • What's a step you could take tomorrow?	Identify small, practical steps they can take immediately toward change

Case Study

Kim, a social work manager in a large, busy hospital, led a team that included doctors, nurses, social workers, and physical and occupational therapists. The hospital administration tasked their managers with addressing the high level of returning patients, and Kim's ward had an especially high number of "repeat customers." Unlike business, in a hospital setting this was not a good thing. Kim called a team meeting.

Kim laid out the issue and summarized what she heard from speaking with team members individually (*Step 1: Acknowledge Problems*): there appeared to be problems with communication, decisions were being made without team input, and the focus on freeing up beds had taken precedence over comprehensive discharge planning. She noted the positive and let the team know that the data showed that when a comprehensive discharge plan was in place, readmissions are reduced by 50% (*Step 2: Describe Success*). Kim also acknowledged the pressure to move patients out of the ward so that new admissions were not turned away. Noting that everyone was busy, she quickly turned the conversation to solutions. She asked the group if anyone had a story about a time when they all worked together well and communicated effectively to get a good outcome (*Step 3: Identify Exceptions*).

Kim paused to let the team members mull this over and then Marci, the ward nurse, brought up Bob. Bob's diabetes was out of control and this past year, the surgeon amputated his right foot. Bob was a prime example of the revolving door as he came to the emergency room on almost a monthly basis for diabetes related crises; he had been hospitalized three times in the past six months. Marci described how difficult Bob was to care for as he was verbally abusive to the male nurses and sexually offensive to the female nurses. Everyone nodded in agreement. Jamie, the ward social worker added that hopefully they seemed to have a good plan for him this time.

Kim asked what was different about the last admission and discharge for Bob. Marci gave credit to Dr. Singh, who was covering for the usual ward physician, Dr. Gerard. Kim explained that Dr. Singh usually worked pediatrics and was not familiar with the adult population common on Kim's medical ward, many of whom were homeless and struggled with alcoholism and addiction. Bob arrived by ambulance after a stranger called 911 when he found Bob passed out in a doorway. Dr. Singh was upset to see Bob's condition and to discover the frequency with which this occurred. Dr. Singh treated Bob and then sent an email requesting a consultation with the nurse and social worker.

During that meeting, Marci and Jamie told Dr. Singh about their frustrations caring for Bob. Dr. Singh asked many questions and, to Marci's surprise, seemed genuinely concerned about Bob and highly motivated to help him. Marci looked at Kim and reflected, "It reminded us that Bob is a human being deserving of our care, and we needed that. I know that sounds bad, but it can be hard to keep trying when someone doesn't seem to want the help."

Jamie explained how despite Bob's unwillingness to talk with her about any personal details, she had worked hard over the past year to get Bob into a transitional housing program with no luck. Jamie went on to explain that they had stopped asking personal questions but that, as Dr. Singh was new to Bob, he asked about his family and Bob mentioned a brother living just 100 miles north of the hospital. When Dr. Gerard returned to the ward the following day, he withdrew discharge orders while Jamie worked on this new lead. Dr. Singh returned to Bob's bedside and got him to sign a release of information and provide a contact number.

Bob's brother was delighted to hear Bob was still alive. At a recent family gathering, Bob's relatives had talked about his struggles with alcoholism and diabetes, and a cousin who worked in a substance abuse recovery program had some ideas for how to engage Bob in treatment if only they could find him. Bob's brother got in his car that day and drove to the hospital. Jamie said, "I'm not going to say it'll be easy for any of them, but I was there when Bob's brother walked onto the ward and I saw the family connection."

The team talked more about Bob and when they were done, Kim asked, "So what happened this time with Bob that we can replicate in the future?" Jamie mentioned how this was a good reminder for her not to become desensitized to human pain and suffering and forget to see the real person behind the injury, disease, or illness. Dr. Gerard agreed that this happened to him as well and that Dr. Singh's attitude and behavior with Bob reminded him of how he used to be when he first started on this ward. Marci acknowledged that she and her nurses found it hard to remain positive but that Bob's story had inspired them to talk about ways to manage stress and counter burnout. Jamie mentioned an article she read about teaching empathy and suggested this could be a future topic for the Grand Rounds and Dr. Gerald agreed to look into it.

Kim noted one thing she heard in the story was that Dr. Singh initiated a consultation and she wondered aloud how often this happened on the ward. The team members talked over each other as they complained about the lack of communication and pointed fingers at one another. Kim quickly jumped in and encouraged them to think of possibilities for the future rather than dwell on the past.

Dr. Gerald noted that he put the brakes on discharge once he knew there was a possible plan and that perhaps they needed a mechanism to

78 *Intervention*

communicate this to him and the other doctors. After batting around various ideas, including posting a big red stop sign and using a pager system, the team agreed to try a new method that required that a "discharge email" receive a read receipt by a doctor, nurse, and social worker prior to discharge taking place (*Step 4: Take a Small Step Forward*). Dr. Gerald was not too happy to share this authority but agreed to try this plan and to meet in two weeks to monitor the outcome. Kim summarized the action plan steps and who would do what to meet the goals of increased empathy, decreased burnout, and improved communication. She praised the team for their candid conversation and expressed how excited she was to meet next time and see not only how the plan was implemented, but also if there were any more good "Bob" stories as a result.

Key Takeaways

- Assume that colleagues want to get along with others and want to make positive contributions to the team.
- Avoid rehashing past failures and instead focus on the present and the future.
- A good solution you come up with today is better than the perfect solution you may come up with in the future.

Discussion Questions

1. Are you starting from a place of believing that your team members want to do a good job and make a positive difference in the world?
2. When exploring problems with your team, are you also focused on ensuring people feel heard and acknowledged?
3. Can your team describe success in a way that isn't just the absence of a problem?
4. Do you ensure that the solutions you develop are within your power to carry out?

References

Carnarius, S. (1976). *Management problems and solutions: A guide to problem solving.* Reading, MA: Addison-Wesley.

Cauffman, L. (2006). *The solution tango: Seven simple steps to solutions in management.* London: Cyan.

Conlow, R. (2001). *Excellence in supervision essential skills for the new supervisor.* Menlo Park, CA: Crisp Learning.

Cooperrider, D., & Whitney, D. (2001). *Appreciative inquiry: A positive revolution in change.* San Francisco, CA: Berrett-Koehler.

D'Zurilla, T. J., Nezu, A. M., & Maydeu-Olivares, A. (2004). Social problem solving: Theory and assessment. In E. C. Chang, T. J. D'Zurilla, & L. J. Sanna (Eds.), *Social problem solving: Theory, research, and training* (pp. 11–27). Washington, DC: American Psychological Association.

Eskin, M. (2013). *Problem solving therapy in the clinical practice* (1st ed.). Boston, MA: Elsevier.

Felgoise, S., & Corvi, K. (2017). Problem-solving therapy. In A. Wenzel (Ed.), *The SAGE encyclopedia of abnormal and clinical psychology* (Vol. 1, pp. 2658–2661). Thousand Oaks, CA: SAGE.

Gingerich, W., & Peterson, L. (2013). Effectiveness of solution-focused brief therapy: A systematic qualitative review of controlled outcome studies. *Research on Social Work Practice, 23*(3), 266–283. https://doi.org/10.1177/1049731512470859

Godat, D. (2006). Random micro solution-focused work. In G. Lueger & H.-P. Korn (Eds.), *Solution-focused management* (pp. 421–426). Munich: Rainer Hampp Verlag.

Godat, D. (2013). Solution focused leadership: The other side of the elephant four distinctions between SFL and SF coaching. *InterAction, 5*(2), 20–34.

Kreitner, R. (1980). *Management: A problem-solving process.* Boston, MA: Houghton Mifflin.

Netting, F. E., Kettner, P. M., & McMurtry, S. L. (1993). *Social work macro practice.* New York: Longman.

Nezu, A. M., & D'Zurilla, T. J. (2007). *Problem-solving therapy: A positive approach to clinical intervention* (3rd ed.). New York: Springer.

Rath, T., & Conchie, B. (2008). *Strengths based leadership: Great leaders, teams, and why people follow.* New York: Gallup Press.

Roseman, E. (1985). Collaborative problem solving; a supervisor and an employee at odds with each other can come together in search of a mutually acceptable solution. *Medical Laboratory Observer, 17.*

Ziegenfuss, J. T., Jr. (2002). *Organization and management problem solving: A systems and consulting approach.* Thousand Oaks, CA: SAGE.

Part Four

Evaluation & Termination

Clinicians and administrators are both accountable to various stakeholders and there is substantial evidence to support the use of frequent and ongoing evaluation and performance monitoring to improve outcomes in both micro and macro settings. This section begins by highlighting staff development as an important focus for the supervisor and manager (Chapter 10), and the closely related topic of performance monitoring through regular supervision and periodic review (Chapter 11). Termination refers to the end of the relationship between client and service provider, which may seem different from termination between employer and employee. However, Chapter 12 will identify some of the commonalities and suggest that some aspects of clinical practice related to termination are relevant for the employee, employer, and co-workers when working relationships come to an end.

10 Staff Development

Once Upon a Time

Rarely in direct practice did I get the chance to work with clients seeking personal growth and development. However, I was able to work with individuals who, once they had resolved the presenting problem to a satisfactory point, wanted to continue to work on other aspects of their lives. For example, a survivor of sexual abuse, after completing a course of Trauma Focused Cognitive Behavioral Therapy (TFCBT), would want additional sessions to solidify gains and push forward with other goals related to self-efficacy. I worked with parents who, after learning positive parenting practices, wanted to work on marital communication and intimacy issues. I worked with families who were referred for homelessness but, once housing was secured, wanted additional support to help improve other areas of their family functioning. Many of these situations required referrals to other agencies or support services that could help clients pursue these goals. I sometimes wished I could work with clients beyond helping meet their immediate needs or symptom relief. As a direct practice social worker, I rarely had the opportunity to work with the "worried well" or the "mildly neurotic," and I never had the luxury of helping clients pursue self-actualization.

As a supervisor and then manager, this changed. While there were serious employee issues I had to address along the way, outside of workflow management and clinical guidance, supervision time allowed for a focus on staff's professional development – the workplace equivalent of pursuing self-actualization. This manifested in many ways. I have a lovely book given to me by a case manager called *Trust*, with an inscription of thanks for helping her to understand her personal issues and then seek outside individual therapy for her previously untreated childhood sexual abuse. I have staff who have not worked for me for years who still reach out for advice on whether to pursue a certain promotion or job change. Moreover, I can survey the social work community in the city where I live and see any number of supervisors, managers, and leaders who have worked for me, and I believe I may have played a part in inspiring them to reach for that goal. Whether it was providing a space to explore personal and professional issues (which are inevitably intertwined when working directly with clients), providing opportunities for training or

84 *Evaluation & Termination*

encouraging someone to pursue a promotion, or challenging them to reflect on their practice more deeply, I thoroughly enjoyed this aspect of my role as a supervisor, coach, mentor, and developer. I hope you do too.

Overture

In counseling or case management, we are often helping others cope with life circumstances that interfere with achieving satisfactory outcomes in multiple areas of their life, including work, play, family, and love. Maslow's hierarchy of needs is a good framework for prioritizing your focus as a service provider. You first focus on food, shelter, and safety, and then move on to securing love, belonging, and esteem in the areas of the client's life where these aspects are lacking. The pinnacle of Maslow's hierarchy, self-actualization, is something that most clients do not achieve or even pursue in therapy, unless they have the luxury of being able to afford psychoanalysis or life coaching.

As a supervisor or manager, your focus is largely on work life, unless there are other issues hindering work behavior and performance (and then you are likely referring staff to an Employee Assistance Program). Gallup's Q12 provides an interesting parallel to Maslow's "hierarchy of needs." Gallup studied millions of managers and organizations, identifying 12 questions that assess whether employees' needs are being met (Buckingham & Coffman, 2016). In organizations where more employees indicated in the affirmative to the Q12, there were a number of positive outcomes including higher rates of engagement, productivity, and retention, which ultimately led to greater profitability. Q12 can be described as a hierarchy with questions 1–2 covering basic needs, 3–6 covering individual needs, 7–10 covering teamwork needs, and 11–12 covering growth needs. These final two questions are the work equivalent of Maslow's self-actualization. This does not mean your employees will achieve a state of nirvana at work, but it does mean that you can have employees who look forward to coming to work each day, find meaning and purpose in what they do, and positively contribute to creating a positive work environment.

The Micro Arena

Supporting a client's development and growth depends on your agency. Maybe your agency provides for basic needs and your role is to focus on immediate relief, such as a homeless shelter, food bank, public assistance agency, or hospital emergency room. If your agency offers the next level of services, such as counseling, education, or case management, these are often designed to prevent the client from needing emergency services by helping them develop life skills to be more independent and less crisis-prone (e.g., providing social skills, financial literacy, emotional regulation, communication skills, etc.). In either setting, you likely have a slew of referrals at hand to distribute to clients to either help them move on to the next level or to prevent them from dropping back into crisis. Social workers in particular are fond of referrals due to their role of care coordinator in many organizations such as hospitals, schools, and integrative care settings.

Few agencies cater to personal development as a stand-alone service. Government or philanthropic entities rightly prioritize their funding for those who are in the greatest need, and personal development is generally considered a luxury. Even therapists in private practice relying on reimbursement from health insurance companies will have to justify services based on a significant mental health diagnosis, medical necessity, or impaired functioning. Some therapists or educators may have an opportunity to work in this area, but interventions such as long-term psychoanalysis or encounter groups designed to foster self-actualization are largely a thing of the past in the United States today.

Some psychology and counseling literature still explores the notion of self-actualization, usually in terms of Maslow's hierarchy of needs and development across the lifespan. In general, self-actualization refers to the notion of individuals fulfilling their potential and can be used interchangeably with terms such as self-exploration or self-realization (D'Souza, 2018). Abraham Maslow is best known for popularizing the term as the ultimate desirable achievement of human development, and his work in this area has been integrated into many human service fields including psychology, counseling, social work, education, organizational management and leadership, community organization, and political and social change (D'Souza, 2018). Today, Maslow's hierarchy of needs and the notion of self-actualization are a part of popular culture and the idea that one is called to fulfil their own unique purpose in life is very attractive to many (Krems, Kenrick, & Neel, 2017).

Krems et al. (2017) studied what self-actualization meant to most people, finding that while this changed over the course of one's life, it was most often linked to seeking status and functional outcomes versus the pursuit of internal subjective states such as happiness. Functional outcomes included having friendships, securing a mate, and caring for others, all of which were found to be central to the individual's notion of self-actualization. This begins to sound significantly more achievable from a counseling or therapy perspective than pursuing an individual's potentially unrealistic idea of living in a state of perpetual self-enlightenment.

Typical interventions used in direct practice to help clients pursue these more functional outcomes may include referrals for additional or adjunctive trainings (parenting class or self-help groups), psychoeducation (stress management or mindfulness), cognitive restructuring (challenging faulty and negative beliefs), encouraging self-reflection (journaling), social skills development, and behavior rehearsal. You have no doubt helped clients achieve increasing levels of self-fulfillment relative to their life circumstances with any number of these interventions and likely more. Other techniques to help clients discussed previously are also relevant to moving clients along this path. We propose many of these will find a place in your supervisory practices to help your employees pursue progress at work for both your own and your organization's benefit.

The Macro Arena

While there are many models of supervision used in human services, they largely share the same fundamental goal of enhancing the quality of the supervisee's work. How you do this may involve a range of activities. The National Association of Social Workers ([NASW], 2013) posited that these activities fall into three overlapping domains: administrative, educational, and supportive. First, administrative supervision is focused on the supervisee's level of functioning on the job. Second, educational supervision is focused on their training needs. Lastly, supportive supervision is focused on managing job stress and building self-efficacy. All three are requisite for effective supervision that meets the needs of the client, the employee, and the organization. That is not to say it is easy to do all three effectively in any one supervisory session – as they are highly inter-related, ignoring any one aspect puts all three in jeopardy (NASW, 2013).

Although professional development is highly valued by employees (Buckingham & Coffman, 2016; Gumus, Borkowski, Deckard, & Martel, 2011), it is too often relegated to the bottom of the supervisory checklist and considered less important or only discussed as time allows. One reason professional development may be ignored is due to the perceived employability paradox, i.e., if we develop our staff too well or too much, they will leave us. Nelissen, Forrier, and Verbruggen (2017) examined the relationship between employee development and employee turnover and put this notion into perspective. Their study showed that even though professional development activities resulted in the employee's perceived increase in employability, this did not influence employee turnover. Upward mobility was considered a positive reason for employees to leave and organizations that supported employees in learning and applying new skills were found to positively impact retention. Employee professional development not only decreases turnover and increases satisfaction, but can also impact organizational commitment (Glazer & Mahoney, 2019).

Professional development comprises a variety of supervisory and management activities, including training, coaching, mentoring, job shadowing, and, of course, regular and consistent supervision. As with direct services, a key factor in these endeavors is the human relationship. Research on coaching has emphasized the importance of the human relationship over any specific intervention done by the coach; empathy, understanding, and positive expectations ranked most highly as critical factors (e.g., de Haan, Calpine, & Curd, 2011; see Chapter 1 for a discussion of the importance of the supervisory working alliance). Even the effectiveness of training conducted by someone outside of the workplace is highly influenced by the immediate supervisor, as they will ensure that new information is transferred and applied at the workplace (Kirkpatrick & Kirkpatrick, 2016).

When it comes to specific supervisory activities, consider combining strategies from the clinical and management realms. For example, Kay Ingamells, a family and systems therapist in New Zealand, combined the use of narrative therapy techniques with the Gallup StrengthsQuest™ coaching model to enhance professional development of social work and nursing students (Ingamells, 2010). She found that not only did all the students report a positive experience but also that by examining their strengths and development in their life history, they had increased confidence in their practice, their academic studies, and their personal lives. Other authors have looked at adapting clinical trauma-informed care approaches to supervision of counselors treating complex trauma to promote clinical growth, prevent burnout, and improve employee retention and well-being. For example, Coleman, Chouliara, and Currie (2018) recommended supervisee-led supervision, providing client services in a context of trauma-informed care, recognizing the signs of trauma in staff as well as clients, infusing knowledge about trauma in policies and procedures, and creating a culture that identifies and avoids re-traumatization. The authors noted that by acknowledging the potential impact of trauma on employees, organizations provide a context for growth and development and not merely survival.

Reflective supervision also contributes to employee development. Ideally, this is a skill set you can quickly develop if you have been a reflective practitioner. While we concur with Beddoe and Davys (2010) that good clinicians promoted to supervisors do not necessarily make good supervisors, we propose that these individuals certainly have a head start when it comes to becoming a reflective supervisor. If you were a diligent student and engaged in self-reflection throughout your studies on human behavior and development, psychology, sociology, etc., you are familiar with reflecting on your thoughts and actions, the influence of your past and current family dynamics, and the impact of your intersectionality and that of others. Moreover, if you took that with you into the world of work, and if you had a good supervisor or mentor as a guide, you probably took time to examine your biases, contemplated client-counselor dynamics such as transference and counter-transference, and rigorously reviewed your sessions, visits, or interactions with clients to refine your skills and expose your blind spots. While reflective supervision is not always included in supervisory or management training, in human services there is the expectation that a high level of self-awareness and continual self-reflection are core components of your regular practice. You should maintain this same attention to reflection on your practice as a supervisor – when you work on your professional growth and development, you will inevitably promote the same in your staff.

Lastly, you should keep in mind that you are also developing future (or current) leaders. According to the Network for Social Work Management (2018), there are four human services management competencies needed to fulfill leadership roles: executive leadership, resource management, strategic management, and community collaboration. First, executive leadership includes professional behavior, communication skills, and facilitating innovative change. Second, resource management consists of human and financial resources. Third, strategic management includes planning, fundraising, and program development. Lastly, community collaboration deals with establishing partnerships and

88 *Evaluation & Termination*

alliances. Your supervision activities should also work toward building these skills in your supervisees.

This Is How We Do It

We often think that sending staff to trainings meets the requirement to provide staff development, and this certainly is a means to teach new skills and fill out the employee's resume. However, your individual supervision sessions with your employees have the potential to make a much greater impact on the employee's performance improvement, knowledge and skill acquisition, and level of professional competence and confidence. The following table uses the NASW's (2013) three domains of supervision as a guide to focus your staff-development efforts.

Table 10.1

Dimension	Areas to Cover	Purpose
Administrative	• Agency policy and procedure • Job duties	Improve staff's level of functioning on the job and work assignments.
Educational	• Evidence-based practices • Direct practice skills • Ethical issues	Enhance staff's ability to provide effective client services.
Supportive	• Professional identity • Stress management • Work-life balance (WLB)	Decrease staff's level of job stress and increase their self-efficacy.

Case Study

When Abeer was promoted to regional manager at a social service agency, she assumed oversight of eight supervisors. One supervisor, Tina, had a reputation that preceded her: she possessed a wealth of knowledge, was an exceptionally skilled case manager, and was highly respected by her colleagues. She also had a reputation as one who did not suffer fools gladly. For the first few weeks, as Abeer focused on getting to know the supervisors on her team, her admiration for Tina grew. Tina had taken just about every possible training available to staff and had binders full of resources and practice tools. She knew the ins and outs of the court systems and had a "connection" at each of them. Abeer began to designate Tina as the go-to person in her absence, giving her the opportunity to walk in her shoes. Although they had briefly discussed professional development during supervision, at the three-month mark, Abeer scheduled a specific meeting just for this topic.

The meeting began by Abeer asking Tina about her career path. She learned that Tina had risen quickly from volunteer to line staff at a family service agency while an undergraduate student. After graduation, she worked at a group home for adolescent girls and soon decided she wanted to pursue a master's degree. She began at this agency as a graduate intern and was hired as a case manager upon graduation. Within two years, she was promoted to supervisor, a position she had held for the past seven years.

Abeer asked Tina where she saw herself in three to five years. Tina shared that while initially she had aspired to be a manager or even director, she was told by someone in senior management that she lacked political acumen and that supervisor would be as far as she would rise. Abeer asked whether Tina would be interested in revisiting her development as a manager, but Tina seemed reticent. Abeer encouraged her to reflect on it and said they could revisit the topic in the future.

At their next meeting, Tina told Abeer that she had thought about it and realized she had allowed one person's comments to stop her in her tracks. Tina told Abeer she admired her communication skills and ability to navigate the political minefields, and that she would like to improve in these areas. Together, they made a plan. Rather than send her to yet another training, Abeer asked Tina to help her adapt a leadership training for their team. She handed off the training binders and within two weeks Tina returned with a curriculum, a training schedule, and a list of potential employees who would benefit from the training. Abeer implemented the training with her team and enlisted Tina as co-trainer. Tina listened intently to the sessions on political acumen and emotional intelligence.

As she was increasingly pulled away to cover another office for a manager on paternity leave, Abeer began to leave Tina in charge of the office more often. Tina excelled and Abeer made a point of reporting on Tina's progress during her monthly meetings with senior leadership. In the months ahead, Abeer continued to mentor Tina and provided her with opportunities to take a leadership role. When a manager position at another office opened up, Tina was encouraged to apply and was chosen for the position.

Key Takeaways

- The overarching goal of staff development is to enhance the quality of your supervisee's work life.
- Investing in your supervisee's development will help them to be more engaged in your organization and the work they do for clients.

90   *Evaluation & Termination*

- Develop your staff so well that they can leave and get a job anywhere but treat them so well that they do not want to.

Discussion Questions

1. When you meet with your staff, which of the three domains of social work supervision do you spend most of your time on: administrative, educational, or supportive? What can you do to strengthen the other areas?
2. How is your supervision approach helping to enhance the quality of your supervisee's work and supporting his or her professional growth?
3. How are you developing the leadership and management competencies of your staff?

References

Beddoe, L., & Davys, A. (2010). *Best practice in professional supervision: A guide for the helping professions*. London: Jessica Kingsley Publishers.

Buckingham, M., & Coffman, C. (2016). *First, break all the rules: What the world's greatest managers do differently*. Washington, DC: Gallup Press.

Coleman, A. M., Chouliara, Z., & Currie, K. (2018). Working in the field of complex psychological trauma: A framework for personal and professional growth, training, and supervision. *Journal of Interpersonal Violence*. Advance online publication. https://doi.org/10.1177/0886260518759062

de Haan, E., Calpine, V., & Curd, J. (2011). Executive coaching in practice: What determines helpfulness for clients of coaching? *Personnel Review, 40*(1), 24–44. https://doi.org/10.1108/00483481111095500

D'Souza, J. (2018). Self-actualization. In M. Bornstein (Ed.), *The SAGE encyclopedia of lifespan human development* (pp. 1921–1922). Thousand Oaks, CA: SAGE.

Glazer, S., & Mahoney, A. (2019). Employee development's role in organizational commitment: A preliminary investigation comparing generation X and millennial employees. *Industrial and Commercial Training, 51*(1), 1–12. https://doi.org/10.1108/ICT-07-2018-0061

Gumus, G., Borkowski, N., Deckard, G. J., & Martel, K. J. (2011). Healthcare managers' perceptions of professional development and organizational support. *Journal of Health and Human Services Administration, 34*(1), 42–63. Retrieved from https://jhhsa.spaef.org/article/1249/Healthcare-Managers-Perceptions-of-Professional-Development-and-Organizational-Support

Ingamells, K. (2010). *Impact of strengths development upon performance and professional aspirations of students in the 'helping professions'*. Auckland: Unitec Institute of Technology. Retrieved from https://hdl.handle.net/10652/1647

Kirkpatrick, J. D., & Kirkpatrick, W. K. (2016). *Kirkpatrick's four levels of training evaluation*. Alexandria, VA: ATD Press.

Krems, J., Kenrick, D., & Neel, R. (2017). Individual perceptions of self-actualization: What functional motives are linked to fulfilling one's full potential? *Personality and Social Psychology Bulletin, 43*(9), 1337–1352. https://doi.org/10.1177/0146167217713191

National Association of Social Workers. (2013). *Best practice standards in social work supervision*. Retrieved December 13, 2019, from www.socialworkers.org

Nelissen, J., Forrier, A., & Verbruggen, M. (2017). Employee development and voluntary turnover: Testing the employability paradox. *Human Resource Management Journal, 27*(1), 152–168. https://doi.org/10.1111/1748-8583.12136

Network for Social Work Management. (2018). *Human services management competencies*. Retrieved December 13, 2019, from https://socialworkmanager.org/wp-content/uploads/2018/12/HSMC-Guidebook-December-2018.pdf

11 Periodic Review and Performance Monitoring

Once Upon a Time

As a manager in a child protective service agency, I was tasked with ensuring, among other things, that initial investigations of child abuse were completed within 30 days. Having done this work myself, I knew this 30-day deadline could be very challenging. Some families were large, parents or other key informants could be difficult to reach, and doing thorough interviews and documentation was a challenge for even the most organized worker. I found two staff members who shone above the rest, with 100% of cases closed within 30 days every month. It seemed like a good idea to have them explain their process and train their peers. Before I did this, I decided to take a look at a few of their investigations.

For one worker, a review of a randomly selected file revealed brief and concise narratives with bullet points and standard phrasing. I viewed another file and it looked remarkably similar. I checked another and began to wonder if she was cutting and pasting all her narratives. Aside from the required interviews with each child and parent, there were remarkably few collateral contacts. Moreover, none of the cases had received any significant intervention apart from a standard referral sheet, regardless of the allegation or the investigation outcome. After reviewing five cases, all of which were closed as unfounded, I looked at the number of cases this worker either opened for voluntary services or brought to court each month: none in over 12 months. This seemed unusual. I then cross-referenced cases assigned to this worker that received another referral within the next 12 months, and found this number to be unusually high. I alerted the supervisor and suggested she look into it further. Needless to say, I did not want this worker training her peers.

For the second worker, it was quite a different story. I read long, eloquent narratives that described thorough investigations with an array of family-specific referrals documented. A review of opened cases showed that this worker spent a lot of time with families, making multiple home visits and collaborating with community partners to ensure families were connected to services. Three cases were opened as voluntary cases and one case resulted in a removal when an unannounced home visit found a sexually abusing parent still in the home. How did she do such intensive services and still close cases in 30 days? I asked the supervisor, who knew her secret: "She works seven days a week, day and night. She is driven to get this done. Three months ago, she had to take a medical leave for high blood pressure. I hoped that would be a message to slow down, but she's back at it."

I did not want the first worker to sacrifice child safety and family well-being for the sake of meeting numbers. I did not want the second worker to sacrifice her well-being for the sake of meeting numbers either. Both workers needed their own specialized intervention. What I discovered below the numbers was a lesson well-learned. Monitoring data is important, but looking beneath the data for root causes can uncover more than meets the eye.

Overture

Monitoring progress in treatment for clients or performance for employees has become standard practice in the past few decades, fueled in part by the accessibility of computerized tools that help both clinicians and managers to collect and track data points and data change over time. Another driver that goes hand in hand with the ability to collect and analyze multiple data sources is the notion of accountability. Clinicians and other direct service providers are increasingly required to demonstrate that what they do is effective in order to continue to receive reimbursement. Human service organizations are similarly required to show funders, donors, and contract monitors that they are being effective. While treatment providers collect data on individual client improvement over time, the agency collects cumulative data to track outcomes for all service recipients. Clinicians have to document weekly progress, draft reports on client progress, and produce final summaries of treatment outcomes. Supervisors track employee performance on a monthly or quarterly basis and then write annual performance reviews for each staff member, documenting accomplishments, progress, and goals for the next year. Managers write up program and agency reports summarizing quarterly, semi-annual, or annual progress toward the agency vision, mission, and goals for various stakeholders. All of these activities serve the same purpose – to keep the target system (client, employee, team, or organization) focused on what is important, provide reinforcement and impetus for continued growth or change, and alert the provider or leader to the potential need for course correction.

The Micro Arena

Most direct service providers and clinicians check in with clients on a routine basis, from "how was your week?" to a more formal review of progress of case plan goals. Many may also ask intermittently for feedback on the quality of the provider-client relationship to ensure the provider is meeting the client's needs. Computer-assisted feedback and monitoring systems that provide continuous evaluation of client progress and treatment outcomes have become increasingly

94 *Evaluation & Termination*

popular, with many providing feedback to both the client and the clinician during the course of treatment to help match best treatments and adjust interventions as needed.

Research has provided significant support for the value of computer-driven tools for the client, clinician, and researcher (Dold, Demal, Lenz, Schiepek, & Aigner, 2010). For clinicians, visualization of progress and discussion with the client are the most important aspects of these tracking tools (Amble, Gude, Ulvenes, Stubdal, & Wampold, 2016). When clients and therapists both have access to ongoing ratings of treatment progress, clients experience significantly improved outcomes at termination (Hawkins, Lambert, Vermeersch, Slade, & Tuttle, 2006). The value of these treatment-monitoring tools is enhanced by the person using them; therapists who are themselves open to feedback, have high self-efficacy, and are committed to implementing formal feedback-monitoring processes have clients who progress faster and are more successful in treatment (de Jong, van Sluis, Nugter, Heiser, & Spinhoven, 2012). Routine Outcome Monitoring (ROM) using a variety of available tools has been shown to predict treatment failure and risk of hospitalization as well as other negative outcomes far more consistently than clinician judgment alone (in fact, clinicians have been found to over-estimate client outcomes and are poor predictors of treatment failure), thus benefiting the client, clinician, agency, organization, and community (Boswell, Kraus, Miller, & Lambert, 2015).

As discussed in Chapter 6, despite the existence of strong evidence to show the effectiveness of several progress-monitoring tools in terms of increased client retention and improvement in treatment, implementation in clinical practice is surprisingly inconsistent (Boswell et al., 2015). While there are certain legitimate privacy and ethical concerns with the blanket use of formal, computerized ROM, the most significant barrier is that therapists maintain high confidence in their own judgment of client progress despite evidence to the contrary (Boswell et al., 2015). As a recent direct practitioner or clinician, you may recognize your own resistance to using such tools. Hopefully, at this point in the book you can look back at the chapters in Section 3 to help you navigate this potential organizational change.

Unless you have worked for an agency that mandated the use of ROM, you most likely relied on informal check-ins with clients or used data dashboards to track process data (e.g., number of client sessions, number of open cases, documentation completion tracking, etc.). These data tools can also be used by supervisors and managers to monitor workflow and task completion. These tend not to measure individual client outcomes as such, but rather track a client's contact with the agency and provide evidence of meeting contract or other agency requirements. Some type of monitoring is required for most direct service providers even if collected via pen and paper and only to determine continued eligibility for services. Regardless of which system is used, in an age of increased accountability, evidence-based treatments, and computerized databases, service delivery of any variety in the human services requires ongoing monitoring to verify progress and service utility.

The Macro Arena

When conducting regular reviews of your staff performance, three common methodologies can be applied: regular supervision, performance-monitoring systems, and performance reviews. Regular supervision includes scheduled meetings with your direct reports – perhaps weekly – as well as ad hoc meetings to address issues as they occur. Performance-monitoring systems include aspects such as electronic monitoring and dashboards. Performance reviews are usually conducted once a year to review progress from the past year and set goals for the coming year.

Chapter 1 emphasized how regular supervision as a process helps to establish a good working alliance. Chapter 10 spoke to the content of supervision (administrative, educational, and supportive). Regular supervision also provides an opportunity for periodic review throughout these domains and provides a mechanism of accountability for the employee, the supervisor or manager, and the organization.

If you did not regularly monitor client progress as a practitioner, this is a practice you will need to embrace as a supervisor and manager. Collecting, reviewing, tracking, and responding to data related to client, staff, unit, team, agency, or community progress is a large part of what you will do. Much like the clinician who is over-confident about their client's progress, you should avoid being an over-confident supervisor. While you may set expectations with your staff, it is best to not assume compliance and instead to inspect what you expect. As Ronald Reagan once said of negotiating with the Soviet Union, "Trust, but verify." We recommend that you use tools to gather objective data to support or refute your subjective impression of employee performance. Furthermore, performance monitoring not only provides an opportunity to influence employee behavior due to managerial action (positive or negative), but also influences the perceived importance of the task being monitored (Larson & Callahan, 1990).

When evaluating and monitoring performance, you can now utilize complex data management systems containing a plethora of data points. Becoming comfortable with extracting and analyzing this data will serve you well, as long as you remember the initial story and critically question the data to best understand the meaning behind the numbers. Data also provides a way for you to demonstrate your team's value to the organization and community. From a more internal perspective, it provides a mechanism to spot problems before they get out of hand as well as a way to identify best practices that can be shared across the workgroup (Ashdown, 2014).

As a supervisor or manager, you will not only want to monitor outcomes, but also examine how those outcomes are reached. Your focus will be on efficiency (whether outcomes were met in the most cost-effective way), effectiveness (the degree to which outcomes were met), and fairness (whether the process is fair for everyone involved) (Ashdown, 2014). This is not unlike clinical practice, where you want to make sure your client meets treatment goals quickly (at the lowest personal cost and the least financial burden), successfully (returning to prior or optimal functioning as identified by the client), and ethically (abiding by professional standards).

Employee performance data should be used regularly in supervision to guide discussions and incorporated into periodic performance reviews. How you go about documenting employee performance may depend on your agency and their human resources practices, but this process can certainly be supplemented with your own attention to progress at more frequent intervals. Over the years, performance reviews have received a great deal of criticism from management experts and researchers. Criticism has ranged from how to make reviews more effective to adopting alternative systems to doing away with them entirely (Holderness, Olsen, & Thornock, 2019). The reality is that the vast majority of organizations use performance reviews (Society for Human Resources Management, 2017) and will continue to do so for the foreseeable future.

We recommend that you review case files *and* make cold calls to clients to ask them directly about their satisfaction with services. Bearing in mind the previous discussion of clinician over-confidence in his or her own judgment and resistance to formal monitoring, it is particularly important that you do this. If you have an employee with an especially high dropout rate, whose clients are slow to progress in treatment, or whose level of productivity is low, speaking directly to their clients can be extremely informative. Receiving feedback may not only uncover egregious employee behavior (e.g., falsified records or unethical conduct), but also provides positive feedback that you can use to praise and reward your staff.

Part of your periodic review should include you seeking feedback from your employees about your performance. In addition to asking employees directly during your individual meetings, you can administer employee surveys, seek anonymous feedback (e.g., suggestion boxes), host a formal employee advisory board, or conduct focus groups. If you demonstrate an openness to feedback by actively soliciting employee input and using this feedback to adapt your supervisory practice as needed, your employees will be more likely to do the same. Furthermore, as monitoring and reviewing progress in treatment improves client outcomes, monitoring and reviewing you and your employees' performance will likely mean improved results for you, your staff, and your organization. At the very least, you will serve as a role model and can shift the culture to one that actively monitors progress through routine reviews and solicits regular feedback from service recipients.

This Is How We Do It

The following table details the three dimensions related to staff performance reviews, highlighting key aspects to cover and their respective purpose.

Periodic Review and Performance Monitoring 97

Table 11.1

Dimension	What to Cover	Purpose
Regular Supervision (covered in Chapter 10)	• Administrative: agency policy and procedure, job duties • Educational: evidence-based practices, direct practice skills, ethical issues • Supportive: professional identity, stress management, WLB	Staff: • level of functioning on the job and work assignments • ability to provide effective client services • level of job stress and self-efficacy
Performance Monitoring	• Monitoring and reviewing the quality and timeliness of their work product • Using tangible data points to discuss performance • Soliciting feedback from service recipients • Soliciting feedback regarding your performance as a supportive and effective supervisor/manager	• Troubleshooting and course correction • Ensure the highest quality service delivery
Performance Review	• Performance goals achieved • Examples of excellence • Areas for improvement • Goal-setting for the coming review period including professional/career development • Feedback regarding how you can best support the employee in his or her work and professional development	• Celebrate the positives and identify areas for growth • Set goals for the coming review period

Case Study

Toward the end of supervision, David checked in with Rosemary and asked if she was getting what she needed out of their supervision time together. Rosemary said yes quickly and got up from her seat to get back to work, but David stopped her and stated, "I know you are busy and you have a lot of things you need to do on your caseload, but I want to be sure I am attending to your needs as an employee and not just the tasks with your clients." Rosemary sat back down and breathed for a moment before she said, "I feel like you are really good at giving advice and pointing out what I need to do, but it would sure feel good if you could identify what I do right sometimes, too." David was shocked, as Rosemary was one of his best clinicians and he thought he praised her often for her work. David was about to list all of the times he had praised her work recently but stopped himself. Rosemary's perception was that she did not get enough positive feedback, meaning David had to acknowledge that what he was doing was not meeting the mark. David instead told Rosemary how impressed he was with her work, and he acknowledged that he needed to do a better job at making sure she knew that. David closed the meeting by stating, "I know you are busy and I don't want to hold you up now, but let's discuss how I can do a better job of this when we meet next week." Rosemary left the office feeling reassured that she could handle the list of tasks to be completed and was pleasantly surprised that her supervisor had responded so openly to her feedback. She reflected on how good it felt to be asked for her opinion and to be listened to and acknowledged. For his part, David made a note to reflect on his use of praise with his staff and make this a topic of discussion with each of them over the next few weeks.

Rosemary had a session that afternoon with a new client for "relationship problems." Recalling her experience with David that morning, toward the end of a session, Rosemary asked the client if the session had been helpful and if they had the opportunity to discuss everything on their mind. The client said yes and began to stand up to leave, but Rosemary invited them to sit back down and asked again if there was something the client hoped to get out of the session that did not occur. The client hesitated then said, "Well, it's been really helpful, but I was hoping you could tell me if my partner is right when he says I'm the crazy one." Despite having what Rosemary thought was a strengths-based intake session – with great dialogue and discussion of relationship dynamics and communication – the client was not as reassured as Rosemary thought. Rosemary wanted to point out all the ways she thought she had communicated to the client that they were not the "crazy one" in the relationship, but instead she validated the client's feelings and assured them explicitly that they were not crazy. Rosemary told the client that while there was no time left this session, this topic would be at the top of next week's agenda. The client smiled with relief and confirmed that they would return next week. Rosemary realized that absent this discussion, the client may not have returned.

Even without the use of a formal feedback tool, asking for very specific feedback allowed David and Rosemary to build trust, engage the person providing the feedback, and prevent disengagement. During their next meeting, Rosemary told David about her experience with the client and they discussed how to implement a more structured process to support the clinicians in asking for client feedback. For his part, David checked in with his direct reports at the end of supervision to solicit their feedback and was pleasantly surprised that as well as getting some specific suggestions for how he could better support the clinicians and staff, he also received a lot of compliments and, overall, he received much more positive than negative feedback. Suspecting that not all employees felt safe giving feedback to a supervisor, David suggested to his director that the agency explore using written or computerized tools to encourage employees to provide feedback to the management team.

Key Takeaways

- Review performance at regular intervals using both objective and subjective data.
- Address performance successes and issues promptly and document these conversations.
- Periodically solicit feedback on your performance from your staff and make adjustments as needed.

Discussion Questions

1. What areas of performance does your organization currently monitor? Where are the gaps?
2. Does your agency solicit feedback from clients to inform performance monitoring and review processes?
3. Do you solicit feedback from your employees regarding your performance as a supervisor/manager?
4. What can your organization to do strengthen its performance review process?

References

Amble, I., Gude, T., Ulvenes, P., Stubdal, S., & Wampold, B. (2016). How and when feedback works in psychotherapy: Is it the signal? *Psychotherapy Research, 26*(5), 545–555. https://doi.org/10.1080/10503307.2015.1053552

Ashdown, L. (2014). *Performance management*. London: Kogan Page.

Boswell, J. F., Kraus, D. R., Miller, S. D., & Lambert, M. J. (2015). Implementing routine outcome monitoring in clinical practice: Benefits, challenges, and solutions. *Psychotherapy Research, 25*(1), 6–19. https://doi.org/10.1080/10503307.2013.817696

de Jong, K., van Sluis, P., Nugter, M. A., Heiser, W. J., & Spinhoven, P. (2012). Understanding the differential impact of outcome monitoring: Therapist variables that moderate feedback effects in a randomized clinical trial. *Psychotherapy Research, 22*(4), 1–11. https://doi.org/10.1080/10503307.2012.673023

100 *Evaluation & Termination*

Dold, M., Demal, U., Lenz, G., Schiepek, G., & Aigner, M. (2010). P02–339—Internet-based therapy process monitoring of psychotherapy using the synergetic navigation system (SNS): Methodology and case report. *European Psychiatry, 25*(S1), 1048–1048. https://doi.org/10.1016/S0924-9338(10)71038-5

Hawkins, E. J., Lambert, M. J., Vermeersch, D. A., Slade, K. L., & Tuttle, K. C. (2006). The therapeutic effects of providing patient progress information to therapists and patients. *Psychotherapy Research, 14*(3), 308–327. https://doi.org/10.1093/ptr/kph027

Holderness, D. K., Jr., Olsen, K. J., & Thornock, T. A. (2019). Making performance feedback work: Companies and employees alike find that the annual performance review no longer provides the timely and effective feedback needed for today's business environment. *Strategic Finance, 100*(8), 46–51. https://sfmagazine.com/post-entry/february-2019-making-performance-feedback-work

Larson, J., & Callahan, C. (1990). Performance monitoring: How it affects work productivity. *Journal of Applied Psychology, 75*(5), 530–538. https://doi.org/10.1037/0021-9010.75.5.530

Society for Human Resources Management. (2017, May 19). *HR professionals' perceptions about performance management effectiveness.* Retrieved December 20, 2019, from www.shrm.org/hr-today/trends-and-forecasting/research-and-surveys/Pages/2014-performance-management.aspx.

12 Termination

Once Upon a Time

One day, Ryan, the program manager for our agency's multi-site after-school program, came to my office looking stressed, closed the door, and sat down heavily in the chair across from me. I stopped what I was doing and asked him what was wrong. He told me we needed to fire Angela, a site supervisor at one of our school sites. He said he had been having problems with her for a long time and she was getting progressively worse. I remembered when Angela was hired a few years earlier and this was the first I had heard of any issues with her.

I asked Ryan for specific examples and he told me about a history of poor interactions with kids and parents, staff who had requested site transfers to get away from her, and ongoing problems with paperwork that had made it difficult for him to put together his quarterly reports. Ryan said he had addressed these issues with Angela many times and wanted me to support his decision to terminate her. I was due to leave for another meeting and had to wrap up with Ryan. I thanked him for sharing all of this with me. I told him I needed to touch base with HR because they had to be on board with her termination. I said I would get back to him by the end of the day to discuss next steps.

Later that day, I spoke to the HR director and asked to pull Angela's file so I could review it. There were no write-ups and no mention of any disciplinary issues – only glowing performance reviews from Ryan, including one from a few months ago. So, what was really going on? Was Angela having serious performance issues that Ryan failed to document? Or was Angela a wonderful employee who Ryan wanted fired for no good reason? Perhaps, it was some combination of the two. Needless to say, when I called Ryan that afternoon, it was not to give the okay for Angela's termination.

Overture

This story points to the way staff development, periodic review, and termination are inextricably – though hopefully not inevitably – linked. Except for extreme cases (i.e., serious incidents that require immediate termination without progressive discipline), the decision to terminate someone must be built upon the staff development and periodic review. But, being fired is not the only way that people leave organizations – staff may leave to accept a position with another organization, they may be unhappy and leave without having another position lined up, they may be laid off due to budgetary issues, or they may leave to enter retirement. Sometimes, the reasons are not clear or may overlap.

Similarly, client services may be terminated for many reasons. Hopefully, it is because the client has met his or her goals and is now functioning optimally. However, as many clients drop out early in treatment, it is likely other causes are involved. Often, we never know why a client does not return for a scheduled appointment and it can range from a failure to connect with the provider to a major life event or even a spontaneous recovery. Sometimes, a client is terminated by the service provider and this may be mutual (e.g., lack of consistent attendance); other times this may not be the case (e.g., inability to pay or lack of progress toward goals).

The reason is important. In direct practice, we can use this information to assess service delivery such as an employee's ability to engage clients, the appropriateness of the intervention model for the identified population, and issues of access and affordability. At the organizational level, the way an organization classifies the employee's separation is significant because each type of exit comes with its own set of management and legal implications.

The Micro Arena

In the counseling and psychotherapy arena, termination is often discussed in terms of premature termination or persistence in services. Unplanned endings, when initiated by the client, tend to be of primary concern, and by some accounts comprise about 50% of overall client drop-out (Hepworth, Rooney, Dewberry Rooney, & Strom-Gottfried, 2017). Premature termination raises questions about the appropriateness of treatment and how it is delivered. The profile of clients who are more likely to drop out suggests that they are the most in need of services (i.e., increased problem severity); thus, counselors are encouraged to try and minimize unplanned endings in order to be able to serve clients at most risk and with higher levels of distress (Saxon, Ricketts, & Heywood, 2010). The factors that influence a client's decision to leave or continue in therapy include several elements that we have discussed in previous chapters, such as the therapeutic alliance, client motivation, effectiveness of the problem-solving process, progress made toward goals, therapist neutrality, as well as time spent on a waitlist (D'Aniello, Piercy, Dolbin-MacNab, & Perkins, 2019; Holm & Barrio Minton, 2016).

Factors that can improve persistence in psychotherapy include setting realistic expectations for therapy and focusing on client engagement (Lucas, 2012). Newer, less-experienced therapists are encouraged to focus on client validation as a behavior that can prevent drop-out and increase persistence (Howard, Altenburger, & Cheavens, 2020). Schindler, Hiller, and Witthöff (2013) found that failure to make improvements early in CBT treatment was a key factor associated with dropouts and they recommended that in addition to considering motivational factors, clinicians should employ the routine use of standardized assessments to enhance symptom monitoring and help to identify clients who are not making progress. Discussions in the chapters on assessment and performance monitoring have addressed the importance of these factors.

In social work practice, termination is categorized into numerous subtypes: unplanned (dropout/kick-out and death), planned/unsuccessful, and planned/ successful (Hepworth et al., 2017). When termination is planned, direct service practitioners can facilitate positive transitions and endings. Evaluation of both outcomes and process can help clients consolidate gains and prepare for future challenges. Even if the outcome was unsuccessful, the social worker has an opportunity to review any gains toward the desired outcome, discuss factors that prevented a more positive outcome, and explore the client's feelings about future help-seeking. The provider is encouraged to be open to feedback and offer referrals for other services if needed or desired by the client (Hepworth et al., 2017). The ideal outcome is that the client successfully completes a course of treatment with goals met and is ready to function independent of the service provider. Sometimes, limits are imposed by the agency, the funding source, or the client's situation. Regardless, consolidating gains and developing maintenance strategies are typically the focus of this final stage of the relationship.

Understanding client (and provider) reactions to termination is also critical, as endings can evoke feelings of grief and loss with related behavioral manifestation of these emotions (e.g., denial, anger, or avoidance), as well as re-emergence of symptoms or problems and attempts to find reasons for maintaining the relationship. In many settings, termination is marked with a ritual that celebrates goals achieved and reinforces positive coping skills.

While rare in the outpatient setting, forced termination or involuntary discharge can be far more common in residential treatment settings. Client behavior that does not conform to the institutional rules can quickly result in the client being "kicked out" or asked to leave. Many facilities will have a list of "house rules" and policies that define consequences for violations of these rules. Depending on the severity of the rule violation, a client or resident may have a number of chances to change behavior or a series of warnings culminating in eventual dismissal. Rarely is this exit celebrated and this is the scenario most akin to an employee being fired.

The Macro Arena

In organizations, termination occurs when an employee resigns, retires, is laid off, or is fired. As with clinical practice, the ending can be initiated by the employee or the employer and the frequency and causes of termination are important to understand. Employee termination is costly for an organization for many reasons including loss of productivity, recruitment costs, and damage to morale (O'Connell & Kung, 2007; Tracey & Hinkin, 2008). When skilled employees leave, organizations lose talent and competitive advantage (Michaels,

104 *Evaluation & Termination*

Handfield-Jones, & Axelrod, 2001). In human services, there is the added cost for the client in terms of interrupted continuity of care and negative impacts on client outcomes. For example, Tremblay, Haines, and Joly (2016) found that staff turnover in youth residential-care settings was associated with increased length of services and subsequent readmissions for clients. For these reasons, human service organizations want to minimize employee turnover and seek to discover what key factors can influence employee retention.

Many of the factors identified in the literature as impacting employee turnover are related to the topics discussed in previous chapters. A centennial review of this research suggested that employers use validated hiring criteria and processes to screen out employees at high risk of leaving, as well as pay attention to onboarding and orientation, as most turnovers occur when new employees struggle to adjust to the demands of a new job (Hom, Lee, Shaw, & Hausknecht, 2017). Major predictors of employee turnover in social work are due to organizational rather than employee characteristics, suggesting that there is much supervisors, managers, and leaders can do to prevent employee turnover (Mor Barak, Nissly, & Levin, 2001). Prior chapters have described how supervisory and management practices can drive employee satisfaction, productivity, and retention (e.g., Buckingham & Coffman, 2016), and this is supported in the literature on employee turnover in social services. For example, organizations that valued rewards for employees and provided supportive and competent supervisors were found to significantly impact employee turnover rates in child welfare agencies (Shim, 2014; Smith, 2005), and higher levels of social support and job autonomy were found to mitigate turnover in social services (Kim & Stoner, 2008).

It is often said that, "employees leave managers, not companies," and with data suggesting that an average employee tenure is one to one and a half years, the pressure is on the organization, specifically the direct supervisor and manager, to engage and retain their hires (Baxter, 2016). While not specific to human services, Baxter (2016) suggested a number of things a workplace can do to enhance employee retention that resemble manager behaviors discussed previously in this book. These include helping the employee feel connected to the big picture to promote a sense of belonging, satisfaction, and purpose; empathic listening to understand and respond to employee motives; validation, praise, and recognition for work well done; and providing employees with a vision for their future in the organization and professionally.

As with client termination, when an employee leaves an organization, people (employee, co-worker, manager, etc.) experience some degree of loss, and repeated losses will take their toll on your team. Rituals and celebrations are a way to acknowledge these transitions and provide opportunities for employees (both those leaving and those remaining) to express feelings, review experiences, and feel valued for their contribution to the team. An exit interview also offers an opportunity for review, and can provide valuable information for the organization.

Although firing an employee will not likely be a common occurrence, when it does occur it can have a significant ripple effect on the organization. This can be positive if co-workers perceive that the organization is dealing with a problem employee who has been impacting their work. When this is the case, employee morale can receive a boost. However, due to the confidential nature of personnel matters, often co-workers are not privy to the reasons behind the forced termination and this can result in morale taking a dip for a while (especially if the employee being fired has the opportunity to tell one side of a situation that cannot be countered by management constrained by privacy rules).

This Is How We Do It

The following table details guidance for navigating employee terminations and communication, and providing support for your remaining team members.

Table 12.1

Party	Voluntary Separation (Resignation, retirement)	Involuntary Separation (Firing, layoff)
Employee	• If the notice is verbal, encourage the employee to put it in writing • Discuss the messaging and timing of the announcement to the rest of the team • Discuss their wishes for any sort of celebration	• Bring a third party (HR or another manager) • Don't surprise the person • Have a clear and concise rationale • Be respectful • Have all your documentation ready
Team	• Communicate the separation sooner rather than later • Discuss any changes in duties/workloads and whether they are temporary • Share the replacement plan (if known or applicable) • Reassure your team and make yourself available to them	• Explain the reason as much as you legally can • Discuss any changes in duties/workloads and whether they are temporary • Share the replacement plan (if known or applicable) • Reassure your team and make yourself available to them

Case Study

Taylor was one of eight clerks who made up the clerical support team for a large social service team in a government agency. She excelled in the job and was regularly praised by the social workers and managers for her productivity and efficiency.

Patrick, the senior clerk, announced his retirement. He had hired, trained, and mentored Taylor, and his departure was difficult for her.

With Patrick's encouragement, Taylor offered to take on senior clerk duties while management looked for a replacement. Leticia, the manager who oversaw the clerical team, recognized Taylor's leadership and suggested she apply for the open position. Taylor submitted an application and after a successful interview was promoted to senior clerk.

The first month or so went well – Taylor seemed to enjoy assigning tasks, following up on assignments, and meeting regularly with the clerical team. She often talked about Patrick and joked about "what would Patrick do" in certain situations. During the third month, Taylor began to call in sick frequently. When at work, she spent most of the time in her office with the door closed. Two of the clerks met, requested a meeting with Leticia, and told her that Taylor seemed angry all the time and it made them nervous to come to work. The same week, one of the social work supervisors told Leticia that Taylor was late with her last three reports and wasn't responding to emails and phone calls.

That Friday, Leticia met with Taylor and asked how she was feeling in her new position after four months on the job. Taylor said "fine" and sat in silence. Leticia asked if Taylor had spoken to Patrick since his departure. Taylor's head dropped and she said quietly, "No. I think he's travelling and I'm sure he doesn't want to think about work." Leticia stated, "I know you guys were close. It sounds like you really miss Patrick." Taylor began to cry. She said that things were going good at first, but now she felt overwhelmed in her role as a supervisor.

Leticia stated, "Do you think how you are feeling is affecting your team?" Taylor's face flushed. She asked if people had been complaining about her. Leticia told her that some people had expressed concerns. Taylor was initially defensive but then admitted that she had been short with her staff and flaky with colleagues. Leticia and Taylor briefly discussed the performance issues, then Leticia said, "I think it's been hard for you to move into a supervisory position when you're still adjusting to Patrick's retirement. And I think you're missing his support and guidance. How can I help?" To Leticia's surprise, Taylor asked if she could demote back to her prior position. She said she didn't think she was the best person to be the senior clerk and that she was happier when she was a regular clerk. Leticia encouraged Taylor to think about the decision to demote for a few days. She said it was normal to have feelings like this during a time of adjustment and also suggested that Taylor consider seeing a counselor with the Employee Assistance Program.

Taylor took the weekend to mull over her decision. On Monday, she met with Leticia. Taylor said that she was in recovery and that taking on supervisory responsibilities while still grieving the loss of a friend and mentor had jeopardized her sobriety. She realized it was also jeopardizing the agency's success. Taylor said she definitely wanted to demote. Leticia was supportive and praised her for being honest and self-aware. Leticia asked if she had thought about how to communicate this with the office. Taylor already had a plan, stating, "I would like to announce it in-person to the clerical team and by email to the rest of the office. I want to tell them that this is my choice and I want to have a job I enjoy and that I miss being a clerk. I think they will understand." Taylor agreed to continue with some of the senior clerk duties but was clear she did not want to provide supervision or lead meetings. Leticia said she would reach out to colleagues in other regions to find coverage for the senior clerk position until a new hire was identified.

Key Takeaways

- Regardless of the reason why a person leaves, other members of the organization can experience some degree of loss and a good manager will be sensitive to this.
- Termination should not come as a surprise to the person except in extreme circumstances.
- Each type of employee separation (termination, layoff, and resignation) has its own set of legal implications for the organization – be sure to follow your organization's policies and procedures as well as state and federal labor laws, including the person's right to confidentiality.
- Exit interviews can provide valuable information regarding strengths and weaknesses in the organization.

Discussion Questions

1. If you have an employee with performance issues, have you discussed them with the person and clearly documented them in writing?
2. Do you give your staff accurate and balanced performance evaluations?
3. How are you supporting your remaining staff after one of the team leaves the organization?

References

Baxter, J. (2016). Why your best employees quit?: 4 reasons. *Talent Management Excellence Essentials*. Retrieved from http://search.proquest.com/docview/1955080226/

Buckingham, M., & Coffman, C. (2016). *First, break all the rules: What the world's greatest managers do differently*. Washington, DC: Gallup Press.

D'Aniello, C., Piercy, F. P., Dolbin-MacNab, M. L., & Perkins, S. N. (2019). How clients of marriage and family therapists make decisions about therapy discontinuation and persistence. *Contemporary Family Therapy, 41*(1), 1–11. https://doi.org/10.1007%2Fs10591-018-9469-7

Hepworth, D. H., Rooney, R. H., Rooney, G. D., & Strom-Gottfried, K. (2017). *Direct social work practice: Theory and skills* (10th ed.). Boston, MA: Cengage.

108 *Evaluation & Termination*

Holm, J. M., & Barrio Minton, C. A. (2016). A predictive model of adolescent persistence in counseling. *Children and Youth Services Review, 67*, 161–167. https://doi.org/10.1016/j.childyouth.2016.06.005

Hom, P. W., Lee, T. W., Shaw, J. D., & Hausknecht, J. P. (2017). One hundred years of employee turnover theory and research. *Journal of Applied Psychology, 102*(3), 530–545. https://doi.org/10.1037/apl0000103

Howard, K., Altenburger, E., & Cheavens, J. (2020). Validation predicting premature dropout from treatment provided in training clinics. *Behavioural and Cognitive Psychotherapy, 48*(1), 116–120. https://doi.org/10.1017/S1352465819000420

Kim, H., & Stoner, M. (2008). Burnout and turnover intention among social workers: Effects of role stress, job autonomy and social support. *Administration in Social Work, 32*(3), 5–25. https://doi.org/10.1080/03643100801922357

Lucas, M. (2012). Counseling on campus: Client persistence and progress. *Journal of College Student Psychotherapy, 26*(3), 227–240. https://doi.org/10.1080/87568225.2012.685856

Michaels, E., Handfield-Jones, H., & Axelrod, B. (2001). *The war for talent*. Brighton, MA: Harvard Business Press.

Mor Barak, M. E., Nissly, J. A., & Levin, A. (2001). Antecedents to retention and turnover among child welfare, social work, and other human service employees: What can we learn from past research? A review and metanalysis. *Social Service Review, 75*(4), 625–661. https://doi.org/10.1086/323166

O'Connell, M., & Kung, M.-C. (2007). The cost of employee turnover. *Industrial Management, 49*(1), 14–19.

Saxon, D., Ricketts, T., & Heywood, J. (2010). Who drops-out? Do measures of risk to self and to others predict unplanned endings in primary care counselling? *Counseling & Psychotherapy Research, 10*(1), 13–21. https://doi.org/10.1080/14733140902914604

Schindler, A., Hiller, W., & Witthöff, M. (2013). What predicts outcome, response, and drop-out in CBT of depressive adults? A naturalistic study. *Behavioural and Cognitive Psychotherapy, 41*(3), 365–370. https://doi.org/10.1017/S1352465812001063

Shim, M. (2014). Do organisational culture and climate really matter for employee turnover in child welfare agencies? *British Journal of Social Work, 44*(3), 542–558. https://doi.org/10.1093/bjsw/bcs162

Smith, B. (2005). Job retention in child welfare: Effects of perceived organizational support, supervisor support, and intrinsic job value. *Children and Youth Services Review, 27*(2), 153–169. https://doi.org/10.1016/j.childyouth.2004.08.013

Tracey, J. B., & Hinkin, T. R. (2008). Contextual factors and cost profiles associated with employee turnover. *Cornell Hospitality Quarterly, 49*(1), 12–27. https://doi.org/10.1177%2F0010880407310191

Tremblay, C., Haines, V. Y., & Joly, J. (2016). Staff turnover and service quality within residential settings. *Human Service Organizations: Management, Leadership & Governance, 40*(1), 22–36. https://doi.org/10.1080/23303131.2015.1085479

Part Five

Self-Care

Some clinicians take on a supervisory role to "take a break" from the rigors of working directly with clients or patients but they may fail to prepare for the rigors of supervision and management. Others may be ambitious and eager to prove themselves, leading to overwork and premature burnout. While moving into a supervisory role can have many positive benefits both personally and professionally, it is a mistake to think that the same attention to self-care and Work Life Balance (WLB) WLB is not needed once direct work with clients is eliminated. This section will explore three very important and closely related concepts related to employee well-being: establishing and maintaining professional boundaries (Chapter 13), vicarious trauma and secondary traumatic stress (Chapter 14), and the often elusive notion of WLB for employees working in the helping professions (Chapter 15).

13 Boundaries

Once Upon a Time

Early in my career, I worked in a group home for runaway and homeless youth as a residential counselor. The shelter was in a regular house and we did our best to help the youth feel like one big family. We had dinner around the kitchen table, helped the teens with their homework, and went on weekend activities together. The staff was also like a family. There were many people in their early to mid-20s and they liked spending time together outside of work. It was a fun group.

I arrived at work one Friday afternoon to find the director, who was rarely on-site, in the office going through files. I asked her if the program manager was off that day. She told me that the program manager was no longer with the organization. I was curious about what happened but thought better than to ask. The director then asked me if I was interested in being the new program manager. It turned out that was why she was there – to talk to me about the position. I said I was interested. She left to head back to the main administrative office to consult with the administrative team and not an hour later, she called and offered me the position. I was thrilled. I always had ideas for how we could improve the program, and now I would have a chance to put them into action. I asked if I could tell people and she said yes. I announced it to the youth and other staff at dinner that night and people seemed as happy as I was.

Near the end of my shift, I was in the office doing paperwork when a few staff members came in. They told me we were going out after work to celebrate my promotion. Cut to several hours later, and a group of ten of us were back at my place after a fun night out. It was well past midnight, loud music was playing, and I was feeling great. Somewhere in the back of my brain, a thought occurred to me: was this a bad idea? I was now supervising everyone in the room. Should I be doing this now that I was the boss?

The answer came a few weeks later when I had to fire someone. One of my staff left the youth unsupervised during a weekend trip. He had a couple of written warnings in his file from the previous program manager and this was the last straw. It was an ugly termination. He was incensed, stating that as his friend I should understand if he had to leave for a few hours and that the youth

112   *Self-Care*

were fine because they were with a volunteer (it was against company policy to leave kids unsupervised with volunteers). He said that I should start worrying about what he might know about me that he could use against me. We stared at each other. I pulled his final paycheck out of my desk drawer and handed it to him. He realized I was not going to back down. He stood up and stormed out, cursing and slamming doors. For several weeks, I wondered what his revenge would look like. Thankfully, it never came. However, I resolved to be more careful regarding the boundaries between my personal and professional lives.

Overture

One of the most significant misconceptions about being a supervisor is there is less need to focus on self-awareness and emotional self-control than you did as a direct service provider. Working directly with clients requires that one be fully present, focused on their needs and interests, and emotionally contained. Doing this day in and day out with clients who often have multiple and complex needs can be draining and contributes to burnout, which we will discuss in the next chapter. This is why some clinicians decide to seek promotion, thinking that as a supervisor they can escape the demands of maintaining such intense self-control and navigating the snake pit of client-therapist boundaries. However, unlike the direct practitioner who can turn this off and on when they interact with clients, the supervisor and manager are likely to be in the presence of their employees all the time (unless in the office with the door shut). The supervisor and manager need to constantly attend to the issue of professional boundaries. This chapter will explore the similarities between professional boundaries with a client and those with an employee, as well as some subtle differences.

The Micro Arena

Boundaries define the difference between the service provider and the service recipient in human services and serve to protect both the client and the provider from potential harm. Boundaries make it clear that the relationship is not social but is rather professional in nature. Boundaries are drawn to preserve the working relationship and avoid ethical pitfalls such as dual relationships, conflicts of interest, and abuse. However, the issue of boundaries is complex, ever-changing, and often resides in a gray area: at times both hard to recognize and easy to violate (Davidson, 2005). Identifying and responding appropriately to boundaries are central to the clinician's training on ethical decision-making.

Despite being fundamental to the helping relationship, practitioners struggle with the application of boundaries. Part of the challenge is the tension between hierarchy and collaboration, professionalism and genuineness, and objectivity and warmness. There is an inherent power differential that interferes with the notion of a true partnership. Being genuine and authentic can be constrained by the demands of maintaining a professional demeanor. Upholding a stance of clinical objectivity can feel cold and distant. Despite these tensions, too often the clinician ignores or minimizes the risks for the client or themselves. Doel et al. (2010) found that only a small percentage of social work practitioners consulted research, professional codes of practice, or agency policy when faced with boundary dilemmas, and that the majority relied on their own judgment without seeking any formal guidance. This is clearly insufficient, as dual relationships (both sexual and non-sexual) make up the majority of ethical violations acted on nationwide by state licensing boards for psychotherapists and counselors (Wilkinson, Smith, & Wimberly, 2019) and over 50% of ethics complaints to the Board of Behavioral Sciences are considered boundary violations (Hepworth, Rooney, Rooney, & Strom-Gottfried, 2017).

Self-disclosure has been described as "the slippery slope" of boundary violations (Hepworth et al., 2017) and there has been much debate in the literature on its appropriateness in counseling and social work. While there may be benefits in terms of reducing the power differential and facilitating connection, it can also blur client-practitioner boundaries and interfere with the focus on the client's needs and interests. Research has confirmed this duality, indicating that therapist disclosure can generate boundary issues and diminish the client's view of the therapist in some situations while enhancing perceived credibility and competence in others (Audet, 2011). Once again, there is no clear direction to the practitioner. Frankel, Holland, and Currier (2012) found that experienced clinicians maintained a strong focus on boundaries in order to attend to the client's needs, to protect their own professional practice, and to empower client self-awareness and personal accountability.

Boundary issues can be unplanned and manageable, such as running into a client in the community outside of work hours or they can be more challenging, such as when the practitioner lives in a small rural community and dual relationships are less avoidable. In such circumstances, purist notions of confidentiality, objectivity, and neutrality can be impractical and problematic (Pugh, 2007). Similarly, being a member of a specific cultural group (e.g., Lesbian, Gay, Bi-Sexual, Transgender, Questioning (LGBTQ), religious affiliation, or uncommon language) can be challenging when working with clients who are also members of that group.

More apparent boundary violations seem self-evident, such as sexual intimacies. However, even this area attracts debate, suggesting that therapists who are too rigid in terms of boundaries may actually harm clients (Barnett, 2014). Although feelings of attraction between client and practitioner will inevitably arise at times, researchers have found that while practitioners generally agree on major boundary violations, they varied in their opinions related to flirtation, fantasy, and touch (Martin, Godfrey, Meekums, & Madill, 2011). Moreover, psychotherapists are generally confused when it comes to understanding erotic transference and how it is managed in the therapeutic relationship (Rodgers, 2011).

A more recent area of controversy for human service providers in regard to boundaries is the increased use of the Internet and social media. Most individual practitioners and agencies have developed specific policies and protocols

114   *Self-Care*

regarding use of social media with clients. Professional associations such as the NASW ([NASW], 2017) have updated their professional ethics and guidelines to provide direction for practitioners on how to navigate digital communication. The opportunities for client and practitioner education, connectivity, and mutual support now abound in the virtual world, as do the opportunities for boundary violations. Managing boundaries across these various domains and media platforms requires the practitioner to maintain a primary focus on the helping relationship and to seek support and guidance from a supervisor on a regular basis.

The Macro Arena

You may think that the easiest way to set boundaries with direct reports is to keep encounters highly formal, share no personal information, and spend no time together outside the workplace. This would ensure that no one gets the wrong idea and help them see you are taking your role as boss very seriously. But setting rigid, broad boundaries like this comes at a price. Recalling the LMX theory discussed in Chapter 1, when managers and direct reports build relationships based on high levels of trust, communication, affinity, and respect (an in-group relationship in LMX speak), employees are more productive, experience greater job satisfaction, and are less likely to leave the organization. Conversely, when manager-worker relationships are overly formal and lack trust and connection (an out-group relationship), productivity, job satisfaction, and employee retention take a hit. The challenge is how to develop in-group relationships while maintaining appropriate professional boundaries.

The supervisor and manager must navigate very similar tensions to those described previously for the therapist. Terms such as authentic leadership and servant leader may suggest a fairly high level of intimacy between leader and follower but being authentic and being a servant does not mean telling all or doing all for your employees. While some level of care must be taken when deciding whether and when to disclose personal information in the supervisory relationship, this decision-making may have different parameters. For example, when a client asks whether or not the clinician has children, a clinician may need to assess whether to respond, "No, but I have worked with lots of parents over the years" or "You are worried that I may not understand your experience as a parent," depending on whether a cognitive (competence) or emotional (connection) concern is at the root of the question. For a supervisor, equivocation about a response to this same question could seem unnecessarily rigid. However, the conversation should not then diverge into a long discussion about the supervisor's family life, but rather should return the focus to the supervisee's workload and need for case consultation. Despite the greater flexibility in the supervisory relationship, the supervisor can still role model through supervision how practitioners can manage boundaries with clients by demonstrating the nuances of providing a safe and collaborative context for an inherently hierarchical relationship that ultimately focuses on the needs of the supervisee.

Self-disclosure during supervision, even when the focus is on work life, still needs to be managed carefully. The supervisor is assumed to have experiences as a practitioner and having supervised others that may offer valuable insights about a situation facing a supervisee seeking consultation. Sharing these stories can be educational and informative but beware of an over reliance on this approach. Maybe you've had a supervisor or manager who repeatedly launched into advice giving with "I had a case like that and what I did was . . . ." Used purposefully, such descriptions of past practice can be beneficial, but, as with clients, repeatedly referencing your personal experiences and providing explicit directions or advice-giving is much less helpful in the long run. The supervisor's job is to empower employee decision-making and facilitate clinical insight or practitioner self-awareness.

For supervisors, seeing employees outside of work and interacting with them on social media can potentially be more relaxed than in the direct practice with clients. It is not uncommon for employees and supervisors and managers to socialize both in and out of work. In our experience, this varies greatly depending on the individual, the organizational culture, and agency policies. Below, we provide suggestions on how to make these decisions in such a way as to protect your privacy and avoid potentially negative repercussions for yourself and the organization. We recommend that like the experienced psychotherapists described in the study by Frankel et al. (2012), the supervisor and manager attend to boundaries to best serve their employees, to protect themselves professionally, and to empower employee self-awareness and accountability.

While it is not uncommon to have romantic relationships in the workplace, these connections can become treacherous once you are a supervisor. Understandably, you should not supervise someone who you are involved with romantically, and most organizations will have clear policies prohibiting such relationships. As in direct practice, the supervisor-supervisee relationship can foster a high level of intimacy over time and sexual feelings can emerge. The supervisor is responsible to ensure any such feelings are not acted upon. Close attention to verbal and non-verbal communication is essential to prevent any appearance of inappropriate sexual overtures, as these can lead to allegations of sexual harassment. This is another reason to be cautious about socializing with employees outside of work, especially when alcohol is present and self-constraint may be compromised. Like with direct practice, this may seem to be a clear taboo that you cannot imagine violating; yet as the "Me Too" movement has shown us, this happens more often than we might think.

A final challenging area for boundaries as a supervisor is if you are promoted within your workgroup and become a supervisor or manager of employees who were previously colleagues and even close friends. In this situation, direct reports may already know a lot about your personal life that may otherwise have remained private. In some ways, this pre-existing relationship can be positive, eliminating the need for rapport building and providing insights about the employee that otherwise would have remained hidden or unknown. In other ways, it can be a potential liability if you assign your friends favored assignments or avoid giving them difficult performance feedback for fear of damaging your friendship. Other employees will perceive this as favoritism, which can greatly damage employee morale. The transition from friend to boss is one of the most significant challenges for new managers (Gentry, Logan, &

116 *Self-Care*

Tonidanel, 2014). Being successful requires clear communication, being fair, paying attention to perceived favoritism, and being prepared for the fact that these relationships may be permanently changed as a result of the promotion (Gentry, 2015). Supervisors and managers, like their employees, need a supervisor, manager, director, coach, or mentor who can help them work through these boundary challenges.

This Is How We Do It

Workplace relationships are necessary to help create a safe and cohesive work environment and for team belonging. Team members need to know something about each other to facilitate healthy communication, understand each other's strengths and weaknesses, and support one another. The question is: Where is the line? What kinds of relationships are okay? Is socializing outside of work okay? What about social media? The following table provides guidance in these areas. Of course, however you proceed, you want to make sure you follow your organization's policies and procedures.

Table 13.1

Dimension	Generally OK	Generally NOT OK
Relationships with direct reports	• When it helps you to create a safe and supportive work environment for all • When you do not feel like you need to hide the existence of or nature of the relationship	• When others believe you are showing favoritism • When your relationship has become romantic • When you are no longer able to provide your workers with constructive feedback, disciplinary action, etc.
Socializing outside of work	• When get-togethers are open to all staff • When you avoid making work the main topic of conversation • Arrive early, leave before the end	• When get-togethers are only for a select group of staff • When gossip is the main topic of conversation • When you are the last one to leave – especially if it is a late night event and people have been drinking
Social media	• If your organization does not have a policy against it • If you are willing to friend anyone in the organization • If your posts are something you would be okay sharing in the workplace • If your settings allow you to approve friends tagging you and posting on your wall before they are made public	• If your organization forbids it • If you only friend certain staff but not others • If you post things that you would not be comfortable sharing in the workplace • If your friends are able to tag you and post on your wall without your consent

Case Study

When David was hired to be a trainer for the professional development wing of a large human services agency, he was assigned to a regional office with two other trainers, Jane and Chaz. These three individuals became close colleagues as they worked side by side to develop curriculum and facilitate trainings. David and Jane shared a passion for food and often went on double dates with their respective spouses. David and Chaz shared fewer common social interests, but they worked well together, and Chaz considered David a mentor and role model.

When the director of staff development announced she was leaving for a new job, Jane and Chaz encouraged David to apply for the position. All three celebrated when David was hired to be the new director. Before he left the regional office, David met separately with Chaz and Jane to discuss the transition.

David took Jane to lunch and they reminisced about the fine dishes they had shared over the years. He said he hoped they could continue to have a friendship outside of work but it might be awkward at times. He explained that he would no longer be able to engage in workplace gossip and some topics would be off-limits. Jane assured David that she understood and wanted both of them to be aware of how other staff may feel about their pre-existing relationship. They agreed to keep open communication as they encountered potential pitfalls.

The conversation with Chaz was a little more difficult. David began by reviewing the great work they had done together and how excited he was to see what Chaz could do with a new co-trainer. Chaz was quick to bring up the possibility of getting a promotion in the near future and possibly reclassifying his current position to "lead trainer" in the meantime. As with Jane, David had to address the fact that their relationship would change now that David was Chaz's boss. David told Chaz he couldn't show any favoritism to him or Jane and had to consider how others in the company would perceive their relationship. Chaz seemed dejected and worried he would be less likely to get opportunities if David was going to be so worried about what people thought. David assured Chaz that this would not be the case and asked Chaz to talk to him if he felt he was not treating him fairly.

This was not the last conversation David had to have with Chaz or Jane about boundaries. There were not many issues that came up with Jane, apart from reminding her occasionally, when out with their spouses, that they could not talk about work. It became slightly more challenging with Chaz. Chaz applied for a promotion and lodged a complaint with HR when he was not selected for the position, ultimately resigning from the organization. A few weeks later, David was pleasantly surprised when Chaz contacted him to share that had secured a management position

118   *Self-Care*

with a refugee settlement program run by his church. He was very excited about this new job and thanked David for not promoting him, stating he would never have looked for a job outside of the organization if he had not been so upset at not getting the promotion. He ended the conversation saying, "Can we go back to being friends now and then I can call you for advice? This is a big job and I really want to be successful." David was pleased to be able to move back into a friendship and mentoring role with Chaz.

Key Takeaways

- Setting boundaries does not mean you have to be cold or detached; if you have no relationship with your direct reports, it will be hard to succeed.
- When the nature of your relationship with a direct report hinders your ability to do your job effectively, the entire organization suffers.
- Even if you believe you can set aside personal feelings, there can be a perception problem among the other employees.
- Bring up a boundary violation right away. Encourage conversations regarding boundaries.
- If in doubt, ask for guidance from your supervisor.

Discussion Questions

1. What are your organization's policies regarding workplace relationships?
2. Which topics/areas of your personal life should never be discussed in the workplace?
3. Do your workplace relationships make it easier or harder for you to be effective in your job?
4. Do you have any workplace relationships that you are trying to keep on the down low? If so, why?

References

Audet, C. T. (2011). Client perspectives of therapist self-disclosure: Violating boundaries or removing barriers? *Counselling Psychology Quarterly*, *24*(2), 85–100. https://doi.org/10.1 080/09515070.2011.589602

Barnett, J. (2014). Sexual feelings and behaviors in the psychotherapy relationship: An ethics perspective. *Journal of Clinical Psychology*, *70*(2), 170–181. https://doi.org/10.1002/jclp.22068

Davidson, J. C. (2005) Professional relationship boundaries: A social work teaching module. *Social Work Education*, *24*(5), 511–533. https://doi.org/10.1080/02615470500132715

Doel, M., Allmark, P., Conway, P., Cowburn, M., Flynn, M., Nelson, P., & Tod, A. (2010). Professional boundaries: Crossing a line or entering the shadows? *British Journal of Social Work*, *40*(6), 1866–1889. https://doi.org/10.1093/bjsw/bcp106

Frankel, Z., Holland, J., & Currier, J. (2012). Encounters with boundary challenges: A preliminary model of experienced psychotherapists' working strategies. *Journal of Contemporary Psychotherapy, 42*(2), 101–112. https://doi.org/10.1007/s10879-011-9189-x

Gentry, W. A. (2015, February 24). Navigating the transition from friend to boss. *Harvard Business Review.* Retrieved from https://hbr.org/2015/02/navigating-the-transition-from-friend-to-boss

Gentry, W. A., Logan, P., & Tonidanel, S. (2014). *Understanding the leadership challenges of first-time managers: Strengthening your leadership pipeline.* Colorado Springs, CO: Center for Creative Leadership. Retrieved from www.ccl.org/wp-content/uploads/2015/04/UnderstandingLeadershipChallenges.pdf

Hepworth, D. H., Rooney, R. H., Rooney, G. D., & Strom-Gottfried, K. (2017). *Direct social work practice: Theory and skills* (10th ed.). Boston, MA: Cengage.

Martin, C., Godfrey, M., Meekums, B., & Madill, A. (2011). Managing boundaries under pressure: A qualitative study of therapists' experiences of sexual attraction in therapy. *Counselling and Psychotherapy Research, 11*(4), 248–256. https://doi.org/10.1080/14733145.2010.519045

National Association of Social Workers. (2017). *Code of ethics.* Retrieved from www.social-workers.org/about/ethics/code-of-ethics/code-of-ethics-english

Pugh, R. (2007). Dual relationships: Personal and professional boundaries in rural social work. *British Journal of Social Work, 37*(8), 1405–1423. https://doi.org/10.1093/bjsw/bcl088

Rodgers, N. (2011). Intimate boundaries: Therapists' perception and experience of erotic transference within the therapeutic relationship. *Counselling and Psychotherapy Research, 11*(4), 266–274. https://doi.org/10.1080/14733145.2011.557437

Wilkinson, T., Smith, D., & Wimberly, R. (2019). Trends in ethical complaints leading to professional counseling licensing boards disciplinary actions. *Journal of Counseling and Development, 97*(1), 98–104. https://doi.org/10.1002/jcad.12239

14 Vicarious Trauma and Secondary Traumatic Stress

Once Upon a Time

When working as a therapist in an outpatient clinic, my caseload was primarily children and adults who had experienced trauma. Several of the children I saw had been sexually abused. One young adolescent (who I will call Kristi) had been raised by her stepfather after her mother died of a drug overdose when Kristi was very young. Although Kristi vehemently denied the abuse, after her stepfather was arrested, the police retrieved numerous photographs from his computer documenting his sexual abuse of not only Kristi but several other children. Kristi insisted the photographs were fake and that her stepfather had been set up by her grandfather (who also had a history of allegations of sexual abuse). Having reached an impasse in treatment, I asked Kristi if she would like to do some art rather than more talking and she eagerly agreed. I brought out the painting supplies and set up the easel and she quickly began lashing on bold strokes of colors. Her painting became more rapid and forceful as she laid strokes of paint on top of each other and then started making circles.

Soon, the colors merged and the paper turned a darker and darker brown. Then, Kristi took the black paint pot in her hand, reached in with her fingers and began smearing the black paint all over the paper. She was visibly angry as she worked furiously to cover the whole sheet of paper. Finally, exhausted, she said she was done and collapsed in the chair. She then looked at me and said, "If I have to believe he did that to me then that means it was only about sex and that he never loved me; and if he never loved me that means no-one ever loved or wanted me and I cannot bear the thought of that."

Kristi was my last appointment that day. I got in the car and headed home to my family. I do not recall the journey other than I was seething with anger. I didn't know Kristi's stepfather or her grandfather but I hated them in that moment. I gripped the steering wheel and cursed their very existence. Close to my home, I heard a siren behind me and pulled over so the police car could pass. To my surprise, the car pulled up behind me. In the rearview mirror, I saw a female cop with a bullhorn and heard "DO NOT STEP OUT OF THE CAR." When she came to the window, I rolled it down and she asked if I knew how fast I was going and why I had not pulled over sooner. Apparently, I had been driving

45 in a 25 mile-an-hour zone and she had been following me with her siren on for four blocks. I had been oblivious. I apologized profusely and explained I had a long day at work and was eager to get home. She seemed relieved and told me that she thought she had a chase on her hands and had called for backup. After issuing a ticket, she urged me to get some rest and let me go.

That evening, after putting my own kids to bed and tucking them in a little tighter than usual, I drew a bath. I lay in the bath and sobbed quietly so my family did not hear me. I cried for Kristi and for all the children I worked with who had been so horribly treated by the adults who were meant to care for them. I began to wonder how long I could do this work without it taking more of a toll on my life.

Overture

Working in the human services field inevitably means working with members of society who have experienced trauma. While not everyone in this field works directly with trauma survivors, most direct service providers interact with individuals and groups who have been impacted by traumatic events whether abuse and violence, medical and health crises, natural or manmade disasters, or societally inflicted trauma of racism, sexism, ageism, and other assaults to the person or group. Hearing client stories and helping clients cope with the aftermath of the trauma is a large part of the work and it can take its toll on the helper over time. As a supervisor or manager, you don't have direct client contact, but you still may hear the stories, review documents that include trauma details, and witness the impact of secondary trauma on your staff. Additionally, you are responsible to provide a work environment that is trauma-informed to mitigate the negative effects of exposure to client trauma. Like the clinician or counselor who provides a safe space for the client to process their traumatic experience, you will need to provide this same safe space for your staff. Trauma survivors benefit from the support of others who have had similar experiences, and, similarly, you can facilitate peer support among your team. Direct service providers also need to connect clients with trauma-informed adjunctive services to help them rebuild their lives (education, employment, healthcare, etc.); similarly, you will need to advocate within your organization for supports and benefits that promote employee health and well-being.

Micro Arena

People working in human services are frequently exposed to trauma. For clinicians and social workers who work with traumatized individuals with the explicit goal of helping them secure safety from further trauma and processing past traumatic events, the exposure to traumatic information can have cumulative impacts on the worker's cognitive, emotional, and physical well-being. Other human service workers are not immune from such exposure, and can often be the unwitting receptor for a client or patient trauma story or response. For example, an employee working in an office providing public assistance may have to ask a parent seeking benefits about domestic violence; a residential services worker

122   Self-Care

working with adolescents may be a daily witness to the sexualized behavior of a youth who was sexually abused or the aggression of a youth who has grown up a victim of family violence; or a court-appointed special advocate may have to read court reports and other documents about their assigned child that include forensic details and physical findings of repeated abuse and unrelenting neglect.

Various terms are used to describe the direct service provider's response to working with traumatized clients or patients. Vicarious trauma (VT), which develops gradually over time, refers to the adverse effects of chronic exposure to secondary trauma on the service provider's emotional and cognitive functioning, personal relationships, and self-perception (Aparicio, Michalopoulos, & Unick, 2013). Similarly, secondary traumatic stress (STS) is a response to hearing traumatic material, but is more acute in its onset and manifests as symptoms similar to post-traumatic stress disorder, such as intrusive thoughts, anxious arousal, and depression (Hensel, Ruiz, Finney, & Dewa, 2015). Other terms often included in discussions of STS and VT are burnout and compassion fatigue. Burnout refers to the emotional, physical, and spiritual exhaustion that often accompanies and exacerbates STS and VT and it can result in a gradual withdrawal from investment in the work of helping others. Burnout is a close cousin to compassion fatigue and refers to the loss of gratification in being able to help those in need (Cummings, Singer, Hisaka, Benuto, & Cummings, 2018).

STS, VT, burnout, and compassion fatigue are often co-occurring and have been found to contribute to several adverse outcomes in the workplace, such as employee turnover, lowered productivity, and decreased job satisfaction (Bride & Kintzle, 2011; Cosden, Sanford, Koch, & Lepore, 2016; Middleton & Potter, 2015). Although working with traumatized clients can contribute to burnout, individual and organizational factors can also influence the likelihood of developing burnout (Mor Barak, Nissly, & Levin, 2001) and can increase an employee's risk for both STS and VT. For example, caseload volume and frequency, as well as the clinician's own trauma history, can increase risk for STS (Hensel et al., 2015). Protective factors that reduce the likelihood of experiencing VT and STS include training and supervision in trauma-informed work (Cosden et al., 2016). Addressing the risks of STS, VT, and burnout are critical to ensure the well-being of the provider and the quality of the services for the client (Aparicio et al., 2013) and thus the prevention of VT and STS should be a priority at the organizational level (Isobel & Angus-Leppan, 2018).

Working in the challenging field of human services is not, however, all doom and gloom. Based on a study of secondary trauma among caregivers working with Mexican and Central American refugees, Lusk and Terrazas (2015) found that despite repeated exposure to migrant experiences of torture, rape, kidnapping, and human trafficking, caregivers and professionals working with this population had high levels of compassion satisfaction (the inverse of compassion fatigue). These predominantly Hispanic helpers described self-care behaviors and protective factors rooted in their family, culture, and faith. Although they reported a certain degree of emotional numbing, they also spoke about increased compassion that came from their admiration of the resiliency of the refugees. This created a sense of hope and optimism and the belief that they were making a difference that served as an antidote for the inevitable toll of repeated exposure to the migrants' trauma.

Macro Arena

Numerous studies have shown vicarious and secondary trauma as significant contributing factors in employee turnover (Middleton & Potter, 2015). In child welfare, where social workers experience high exposure to trauma, turnover rates are especially high, with some agencies reporting rates as high as 65% (Casey Family Programs, 2019). Turnover has a significant impact on the organization, remaining staff, and vulnerable clients. When workers leave, the cost to the organization can be from 30% up to 200% of the employee's salary (CPS Human Resource Services, 2006). Remaining staff are at higher risk of burnout and compassion fatigue due to higher workloads, thus becoming increasingly vulnerable to VT and STS (Cummings, Singer, Hisaka, Benuto, & Cummings, 2018). Vulnerable clients and patients experience decreased availability and quality of services from staff turnover, which has been associated with poorer client outcomes (Flower, McDonald, & Sumski, 2005).

Interventions for STS and VT are not necessarily the same for the practitioner as for the client who experienced the trauma but this is an area that needs additional research (Bercier & Maynard, 2014). Self-care practices are often recommended for healing or protection from the effects of vicarious or secondary trauma, though there is also minimal empirical research regarding their efficacy. Training in VT and STS is another common organizational response, but training alone is not enough and treatment providers also need opportunities to develop personal and professional supports (Cosden et al., 2016).

Joubert, Hocking, and Hampson (2013) conducted an exploratory study of oncology social workers in a fast-paced, acute care hospital where social workers experienced high levels of exposure to patient trauma. The study participants emphasized the important role of regularly scheduled professional supervision that not only focused on theory and practice but also addressed the emotional impact on the practitioner and helped navigate the workload and the organization. They also placed a high value on the informal support of peers and the ways in which the organization supported and promoted opportunities for peer interaction. Other organizational factors that were designed to mitigate employee exposure to trauma were the ability to take time off monthly, access to an Employee Assistance Program, and personal and professional development opportunities such as subsidized yoga, massages, and leadership development programs.

Houston-Kolnik, Odahl-Ruan, and Greeson (2017) explored the role of formal and informal supports for rape crisis advocates and found that advocates valued opportunities to emotionally process their experiences. In this study, opportunities for debriefing with peers in the workplace were emphasized, noting the sensitive nature of the trauma (rape) and the lack of sensitivity or knowledge of how to respond by those outside of the organization or profession.

Becoming a trauma-informed organization has been shown to lower STS, burnout, and compassion fatigue as well as improve key workforce performance

124   *Self-Care*

indicators, translating into better outcomes for clients (Child Health and Development Institute of Connecticut, 2016). Being a trauma-informed agency recognizes the impact of the organization and the system on the individual or family as well as the impact of trauma and stress on the caseworker or clinician (Heffernan & Viggiani, 2015). Casey Family Programs (2010) recommended a number of strategies organizations can use to become trauma-informed, including staff involvement (Trauma-Informed Staff Committee); staff development and training; creating a safety culture (high levels of communication and transparency); upgrades to the work environment (calming colors, inspiring artwork, or good lighting); and peer support.

In this book, the authors have frequently addressed the importance of the supervisor and manager as role models for the workforce. This is especially true when it comes to practicing behaviors that demonstrate self-care, healthy coping skills, and advocating for organizational supports to meet worker needs. Such behaviors can also protect supervisors from STS due to lack of organizational support, which can interfere with their capacity to support their direct reports (Dombo & Blome, 2016). Managers and leaders of organizations who deliver services to traumatized clients and patients can conduct an organizational audit focused on workforce well-being and identify the types of organizational supports that mitigate the negative effects of exposure to secondary trauma (Dombo and Blome, 2016).

This Is How We Do It

The following table details various types of interventions along with corresponding activities to address STS and VT.

Table 14.1

Level of Intervention	Activities to Prevent or Respond to STS and VT
Formal supports	• Training on STS and VT • Regularly scheduled individual supervision that provides a safe space for employees to process the impact of exposure to traumatic material • Group supervision that promotes a sense of teamwork
Informal supports	• Opportunities for peer debriefing • Employee-focused social events • Peer mentoring programs
Organizational supports	• Employee Assistance Program • Subsidized yoga, massages, and gym memberships • Balanced workload • Leadership development and other professional development opportunities • Regular time off, e.g., approved "mental health" days • Organizational culture that promotes WLB

Case Study

As a new supervisor at an agency serving severely mentally ill clients, Sam provided oversight of an inter-disciplinary team consisting of job coaches, social workers, psychologists, nurses, and contract psychiatrists. When Sam was hired, she was told by her new manager that she would need to focus on productivity and outcomes, as her team was trailing other clinics in these areas. Sam had many ideas about how the team could work more efficiently and she identified several key training needs. However, Sam sensed a high level of distrust and disengagement, and the few suggestions she made during individual and team meetings were met with resistance or outright rejection.

Prior to the next team meeting, Sam asked everyone to plan on extending their regular meeting time by an additional hour, letting staff know that she wanted to use this extra time to get to know them as a team and better understand their strengths and needs. Sam asked each team member to be prepared to share their work experiences at the agency as well as something outside of work that was important to them. Sam listened, reflected, and asked clarifying questions as each team member spoke and she soon learned that most team members were frustrated with a management team that they felt did not appreciate the challenges they faced. They were upset about the frequent memos, emails, and lectures from upper management about their poor statistics and they thought the prior supervisor left because of this pressure and lack of management support. They talked about the increasing rates of homelessness among their clientele, resulting in constant crises and high no-show rates. They described frequent absences from the contract psychiatrists, leaving clients without needed medication and jeopardizing their recovery. They talked about the impact of opioid addiction on some long-term clients, several of whom had died of overdoses in the past year.

Sam soon realized that the team was highly connected to the community they served and had been devastated to witness such loss and hardship for their clients. She also picked up on a high level of fatigue among team members, both emotionally and physically. She had reviewed personnel records and knew there was high employee turnover among new hires, but that over half of the clinic employees had worked at the clinic for over five years. She had also discovered that two team members had been on medical leave for over two months, and the remaining members were struggling to absorb their caseload.

Sam asked the miracle question and heard a vision of clients having shelter, access to medically assisted treatment for opioid addiction, regular psychiatric care, and that team members come to work feeling hopeful for the future. She listened intently and reflected back what she heard. The team members nodded their heads and the nurse stated, "Yes, there you have it – I think you understand now." Sam asked what it would take to get there. Though she had many ideas she wanted to contribute, she sat silently, knowing that she needed to allow the team to identify potential solutions. Eventually, one of the social workers said, "I would like to attend the city task force on housing and homelessness. I want to advocate at a systems level for our clients. I know that takes me away from the clinic once a month, but at least I'd feel like I was doing something about the larger issues at play." Gradually, each team member threw out ideas. The nurse suggested they reclassify the open nursing position as a nurse practitioner who can prescribe medications and install telehealth equipment to provide psychiatric care remotely. She suggested training everyone on opioid use disorder and asked Sam to advocate with management to consider integrating medication-assisted treatment at the clinics. The psychologist addressed the loss of clients to overdoses, suicide, and health conditions exacerbated by homelessness. He shared how hard it had been personally on him and wondered if the agency would consider hiring an external facilitator to provide some training on secondary and vicarious trauma. He also suggested that some team members might benefit from individual counseling as they had their own personal experiences of trauma and loss that impacted their ability to cope with their experiences with clients.

Sam then asked the team what was working well. She acknowledged that the work they did at the clinic was very demanding – they had to manage high caseloads; respond to perpetual crises; bear witness to the traumatic life experiences of people without homes, health, or hope; and come back to work every day ready to listen and care for individuals the rest of society had given up on. Sam asked how they did it. The team members looked at one another and smiled and several in unison said, "We've got each other." One by one, team members shared about the value of having peers that listened to them, of the Friday lunch pizza parties, of the weekly walk and talk group, and about the relationships they had with one another that served as a buffer against the emotional impact of the work. Sam was impressed with the sense of camaraderie and told them so.

The meeting ran long but Sam was able to wrap up with a list of items identified by the team by priority and each team member volunteered to work on at least one item before they met again in two weeks. Sam felt a new sense of hope in the room and perhaps some trust in her as their new leader. She also had a list of requests to take back to her manager. Sam gathered together some information on compassion fatigue and employee burnout and how to create a trauma-informed workplace and was ready to educate the organization.

Key Takeaways

- Secondary exposure to trauma by service providers, if not addressed, can result in VT, STS, and burnout, compromising employee well-being, client care, and employee retention.
- The psychological, emotional, and physical effects of VT and STS include symptoms common to post-traumatic stress disorder such as hyperarousal, intrusive thoughts, disrupted sleep, and depression.
- Regular quality supervision that provides a safe space for employees to process exposure to traumatic material and training about STS and VT can mitigate negative impacts.
- Organizations can create workplaces that prevent and respond effectively to trauma exposure, such as balancing caseloads, promoting opportunities for formal and informal support, and adopting trauma-informed policies that support a healthy WLB.

Discussion Questions

1. Do you provide regular supervision that includes the opportunity to discuss exposure to traumatic material?
2. Do you feel prepared to discuss VT and STS with your direct reports?
3. Does your organization provide training in STS and VT?
4. How are you impacted by trauma in the workplace and what coping strategies do you employ?

References

Aparicio, E., Michalopoulos, L., & Unick, G. (2013). An examination of the psychometric properties of the Vicarious Trauma Scale in a sample of licensed social workers. *Health & Social Work, 38*(4), 199–206. https://doi.org/10.1093/hsw/hlt017

Bercier, M. L., & Maynard, B. R. (2014). Interventions for secondary traumatic stress with mental health workers. *Research on Social Work Practice, 25*(1), 81–89. https://doi.org/10.1177/1049731513517142

Bride, B., & Kintzle, S. (2011). Secondary traumatic stress, job satisfaction, and occupational commitment in substance abuse counselors. *Traumatology, 17*(1), 22–28. https://doi.org/10.1177/1534765610395617

Casey Family Programs. (2019). *How does turnover affect outcomes?* Retrieved from www.casey.org/turnover-costs-and-retention-strategies/

Child Health and Development Institute of Connecticut. (2016). *Building a trauma-informed child welfare system (CONCEPT).* Retrieved from www.chdi.org/index.php/publications/issue-briefs/issue-brief-49

Cosden, M., Sanford, A., Koch, L. M., & Lepore, C. E. (2016). Vicarious trauma and vicarious posttraumatic growth among substance abuse treatment providers. *Substance Abuse, 37*(4), 619–624. https://doi.org/10.1080/08897077.2016.1181695

CPS Human Resource Services. (2006). *The turnover toolkit: A guide to understanding and reducing employee turnover: Tool 1: Calculating the cost of employee turnover* [Excerpted chapter]. Retrieved from http://ncwwi.org/files/Retention/Calculating_the_cost_of_Employee_Turnover.pdf

128 *Self-Care*

Cummings, C., Singer, J., Hisaka, R., Benuto, L., & Cummings, C. (2018). Compassion satisfaction to combat work-related burnout, vicarious trauma, and secondary traumatic stress. *Journal of Interpersonal Violence*. https://doi.org/10.1177/0886260518799502

Dombo, E. A., & Blome, W. W. (2016). Vicarious trauma in child welfare workers: A study of organizational responses. *Journal of Public Child Welfare, 10*(5), 505–523. https://doi.org/10.1080/15548732.2016.1206506

Flower, C., McDonald, J., & Sumski, M. (2005). *Review of turnover in Milwaukee county private agency child welfare ongoing case management staff.* Retrieved from https://uh.edu/socialwork/_docs/cwep/national-iv-e/turnoverstudy.pdf

Heffernan, K., & Viggiani, P. (2015). Going beyond trauma informed care (TIC) training for child welfare supervisors and frontline workers: The need for system wide policy changes implementing TIC practices in all child welfare agencies. *The Advanced Generalist: Social Work Research Journal, 1*(3/4), 36–58. https://soar.wichita.edu/dspace/handle/10057/585

Hensel, J., Ruiz, C., Finney, C., & Dewa, C. (2015). Meta-analysis of risk factors for secondary traumatic stress in therapeutic work with trauma victims. *Journal of Traumatic Stress, 28*(2), 83–91. https://doi.org/10.1002/jts.21998

Houston-Kolnik, J. D., Odahl-Ruan, C. A., & Greeson, M. R. (2017). Who helps the helpers? Social support for rape crisis advocates. *Journal of Interpersonal Violence*. Advance online publication. https://doi.org/10.1177/0886260517726970

Isobel, S., & Angus-Leppan, G. (2018). Neuro-reciprocity and vicarious trauma in psychiatrists. *Australasian Psychiatry, 26*(4), 388–390. https://doi.org/10.1177%2F1039856218772223

Joubert, L., Hocking, A., & Hampson, R. (2013). Social work in oncology-managing vicarious trauma: The positive impact of professional supervision. *Social Work in Health Care, 52*(2–3), 296–310. https://doi.org/10.1080/00981389.2012.737902

Lusk, M., & Terrazas, S. (2015). Secondary trauma among caregivers who work with Mexican and Central American refugees. *Hispanic Journal of Behavioral Sciences, 37*(2), 257–273. https://doi.org/10.1177/0739986315578842

Middleton, J. S., & Potter, C. C. (2015). Relationship between vicarious traumatization and turnover among child welfare professionals. *Journal of Public Child Welfare, 9*(2), 195–216. https://doi.org/10.1080/15548732.2015.1021987

Mor Barak, M. E., Nissly, J. A., & Levin, A. (2001). Antecedents to retention and turnover among child welfare, social work, and other human service employees: What can we learn from past research? A review and metanalysis. *Social Service Review, 75*(4), 625–661. https://doi.org/10.1086/323166

15 Work–Life Balance

Once Upon a Time

I delayed parenthood for several years, worried that my passion for my work and my career goals were incompatible with being a parent. Then one day, a lightbulb went off. I was raised by two full-time working parents and I had turned out OK (more or less!). Worries bubbled up again when I was pregnant with my first child. How could I love all the kids on my caseload and still have room left in my heart for my son? Before I went on maternity leave, I requested a transfer to a "desk job" and was ready to invest all my time and energy into my newborn.

I took four months off work to bond with my son and the first three months were wonderful. By the fourth month, I was feeling restless. I started calling my colleagues who had absorbed my caseload to find out how the kids were doing. I was reading the professional journals again and I was ready to be back at work. The new position entailed fielding consumer and community complaints and writing proposed changes to policies and practice protocols based on stakeholder feedback. For the first time ever in my social work career, I left work on time, did not think of work at the weekend, and sometimes sat at my desk with nothing to do. I felt guilty as I saw my colleagues running around dealing with burgeoning caseloads and constant client crises. I also got bored. I was struggling to find the right balance between my life at home and my life at work.

This balancing act has been ongoing. Neither work nor home have a monopoly on feelings of guilt, pleasure, exhaustion, and joy – I find them at both places. Even now, with both my sons grown and off at college, my dog is looking at me and wondering when I am going to stop tapping this keyboard and take her for a walk. I know that walk will be good for both of us, but I am also enjoying the writing and am very aware of the looming publisher's deadline. WLB is an individual quest and looks different for each of us at different times in our lives.

Overture

While working in human services is meaningful and rewarding, it comes with many pressures. The hours can be long and unpredictable, often requiring emergency or on-call status. We deal with people when they are suffering the

130   *Self-Care*

most. The commitment needed for this type of work often leads to the blurring of boundaries between work and home; it is hard to walk away from a person in need when your vocation is to be a helper. Then there is the added influence of the environmental context of working in this field. Political changes impact funding sources and social priorities; global changes such as wars, migration, and climate change affect or create vulnerable populations and new societal challenges; and increased access via cell phones and laptops leads to the demand for instant responses and quick fixes. It is no wonder WLB for social workers has been described as elusive (Fouché & Martindale, 2011).

WLB is equally elusive for supervisors and managers, but as the role models for your staff, once again, you have to rise to the occasion and show them how it is done. You play a significant role in helping your employees craft their own version of WLB through strong and supportive supervision and acting as a buffer between the staff person and the larger organization. The advocacy skills you have used on behalf of clients will now come into play as you work with your agency leaders to create a workplace that employs practices and policies that promote a balance between paid work and life outside of work for your employees.

Micro Arena

Employment is good for us. There is ample research that shows the benefits of being engaged in meaningful work for both physical and mental health and well-being (Isaacs, 2012). However, it is also the case that poor quality employment and stressful workplaces can be detrimental to an employee's health. Those who choose to work in social work and other helping professions usually find their work meaningful, but job satisfaction is compromised by high caseloads, poor supervision, lack of career opportunities, and lack of autonomy (Kalliath & Kalliath, 2015). Social work has been described as the most overeducated and underpaid workforce; while social workers do not pursue the profession for the money, low wages and limited earning potential reflect the value society places on this service and can further erode job satisfaction.

WLB and work-life conflict (WLC) are intertwined with job satisfaction. Human service providers have a life outside of work and the influence of family on work and work on family is bi-directional; work pressures interfere with family functioning and family pressures contribute to conflict at work. WLC is associated with a host of problems such as depression, anxiety, hypertension, somatic problems, substance abuse, emotional exhaustion, marital tension, and family disruption (Jang, Zippay, & Jang, 2011). Many clinicians and direct service practitioners address the issue of WLC with clients and strive to help them achieve a better WLB, the latter of which refers to the successful integration of family and work time with minimal role conflict. Integration is proposed as a better goal than balance as the satisfactory state, for each individual may differ at different times in their professional trajectory and there may not be an equal division of time and energy between home and work (Jang et al., 2011).

There are strategies individuals can employ to better manage the boundary between work and home, and, when successful, employees can focus more at work, be more efficient and effective, and leave on time with less stress (Kossek & Lautsch, 2008). These strategies include using a personal alarm to indicate that it is time to wrap up and transition, scheduling time buffers when moving from one task to another, pacing the work, and regular physical exercise (Ernst Kossek, Kalliath, & Kalliath, 2012). Developing cultural intelligence is another recommendation; Rao (2017) suggested that work and life have two different cultures, and being able to move deftly between the two can play a role in preventing the stress and negative outcomes of WLC.

However, many factors affecting WLB are rooted in the organizational context (Fouché & Martindale, 2011). High and demanding caseloads, excessive paperwork, and insufficient training are beyond the individual's control. The concept of WLB is something the employer needs to embrace if employees are going to have the opportunities needed to craft their own version of a healthy balance between time at work and time for other life obligations.

Macro Arena

Supervisor stress also impacts physical and mental health, WLB, and development of unhealthy behaviors. When work disrupts family and social life for supervisors and managers this is concerning because a good home life protects from stresses at work. As with employee work stress, organizational and personal behaviors can impact coping for supervisors (Griffiths, Harper, Desrosiers, Murphy, & Royse, 2019). The bi-directional nature of work-family conflict, where work pressures interfere with family functioning and family pressures contribute to conflict at work, suggest that organizational policies should support all employees across the organization in managing their family commitments responsibly (Kalliath & Kalliath, 2015). Support for supervisors is critical as their capacity to provide good supervisory support positively influences WLB, job satisfaction, life satisfaction, organizational commitment, and job performance for their direct reports (Talukder, Vickers, & Khan, 2018). This in turn has implications for employee turnover and workplace stress.

Wu, Rusyidi, Claiborne, and McCarthy (2013) studied child welfare workers and found that while job-related factors such as job value, organizational support, and work hours contributed to WLB, supervisor and workplace support was a mitigating influence. The challenge for supervisors and managers is to manage employee stress and burnout in order to ensure quality services and employee retention. Many recommendations found in this book help meet this charge, such as a quality orientation, supervision, workflow management, professional development, use of praise and recognition, and reflective practices and self-awareness. Additionally, like the supervisor's response to STS and VT described in Chapter 14, supervisors need to provide a work climate where service providers can discuss their worries about work and home life and seek help in reducing conflict (Lambert, Pasupuleti, Cluse-Tolar, Jennings, & Baker, 2006).

132 *Self-Care*

For some supervisors in human services, providing this type of support for staff can feel like swimming against the current. Far too often, the issues are rooted in various aspects of the organization and in the context of service delivery; these are the real stressors that impact job satisfaction, professional commitment, and employee retention. These stressors include staff shortages and demanding workloads, excessive paperwork and administrative burdens, limited resources, and inadequate training. It is easy to see how the stress can become "indescribable" as reported by the frontline supervisors in a study of state child welfare agencies (Griffiths et al., 2019).

WLB practices are becoming more popular due to their value to both employees and employers. Promoting a healthy WLB improves employee outcomes such as commitment, motivation, and retention, which in turn leads to increased organizational outcomes (Sánchez-Vidal, Cegarra-Leiva, & Cegarra-Navarro, 2012). Unfortunately, management and staff may have quite different perceptions about the availability of WLB practices; those lower in the organizational hierarchy may have less access to flexible schedules or working from home, some available supports may not be promoted by management, and often employees only seek out such support when they need it (e.g., when starting a family or becoming a caregiver; Sánchez-Vidal et al., 2012). Failing to provide and promote WLB practices can affect an organization's capacity to reach desirable outcomes.

Gravador and Teng-Calleja (2018) described WLB crafting behaviors such as protecting private time, working efficiently, and fostering family relationships that are associated with higher WLB. They suggested that organizations support individual efforts to master crafting behaviors by allowing flexibility in socialization, productivity, and time management. Authentic leadership is also proposed as a mediator if the leader role models good WLB (Braun & Peus, 2018).

This Is How We Do It

Actions taken by the individual, the supervisor or manager, and organizational leadership can promote or compromise employee WLB. The following table details considerations for each level of the organization.

Table 15.1

Level of Intervention	Activities Promoting Healthy WLB
Individual	• Use a timer or other reminder to allow time to transition from work to home • Take regular vacations and time away from the office • Use supervision to discuss potential impact of work stressors at home and home stressors that may impact work
Supervisor/ Manager	• Role model WLB • Provide expectations for WLB during orientation and training and educate employees about available resources and supports • Be prepared to discuss WLB and WLC in supervision

(Continued)

Table 15.1 (Continued)

Level of Intervention	Activities Promoting Healthy WLB
Organizational Leader	• Promote behaviors positively impacting WLB • Provide opportunities for flexible work schedules, teleworking, and other workplace adaptations that support WLB • Review administrative requirements and documentation demands to assess relevance and consider eliminating or reducing "red tape" • Use data-driven practices to monitor workload, staffing levels, and training needs

Case Study

The Department of Mental Health had a strict rule about employee transfers – not before the clinician had completed two years in their current assignment. Yeni was assigned to the HIV/AIDS clinic 35 miles from her home and was initially very happy. Yeni was single and lived at home with her mother and grandmother. Yeni's father was out of the picture and her grandfather had died when she was a teenager. Since then, the three generations of women had settled into a comfortable routine living together.

Fourteen months after Yeni started at the clinic, her mother was in a serious car accident that resulted in her being paralyzed from the neck down and suffering a substantial brain injury. Yeni's life turned upside down as she had to advocate for her mother's care, navigate the health insurance system, and take over all financial responsibility for the family. Yeni's grandmother was also in poor health and could not work or drive, so it all fell on Yeni. Yeni took some leave to set things up at home, but she returned to work as soon as she could in fear that she would lose her job if she was out too long.

Yeni's supervisor, James, was concerned that she was back at work so quickly. During supervision, James asked how she was doing and Yeni burst into tears. She said she had no idea how she was going to care for both her mother and grandmother. Her commute added an extra two hours to her workday and she could not go home at lunch to check on them. James provided Yeni with information about the Family Medical Leave Act (FMLA) and suggested that she speak with someone at HR to find out what other benefits and resources might be available for Yeni and her family. James reassured Yeni that he would find coverage for her cases if she needed to take time off. James told her that she needed to take care of herself before she could take care of others and reminded her how he had taken nearly a month off when his child was sick last winter.

134 *Self-Care*

Yeni then asked if she could transfer to the outpatient mental health clinic that was nearer to her home so she could be close by if there was an emergency. James knew that the county government tended to be very rigid about their rules and had to be honest with Yeni that this might not be possible. The next day, James met with his manager and told them about Yeni's situation. He made the case why the rule should be waived in Yeni's case due to her family situation. The manager agreed to petition the director on Yeni's behalf. To everyone's surprise, the director agreed to the transfer. The director also sent Yeni a personal message of condolences and encouraged her to take the time she needed to care for her family.

A year later, Yeni had established a routine at home. She was able to provide morning and evening care for her mother and had hired a neighbor to come in and check on her mother and grandmother throughout the day. She enjoyed her work at the new clinic, where she had taken on additional responsibilities as an intern coordinator. Yeni also became a resource for the other clinicians whenever anyone had a question about FMLA, health insurance, or in-home supportive services. Being a consumer of services had opened Yeni's eyes to the challenges of accessing and coordinating services and she believed she was a better clinician due to her personal experience. Yeni was forever grateful for James' advocacy and felt valued as an employee.

Key Takeaways

- Work-Life Balance (WLB) looks different for different people at different times, so provide opportunities to talk with each individual about what they need to craft their optimum WLB plan.
- Since supervisory stress can negatively impact employees, seek your own supervision and support to find your best version of WLB.
- While there are actions that individuals can take to better cope with Work-Life Conflict (WLC), many barriers to achieve WLB are organizational in nature, so be prepared to advocate for WLB policies at your agency or workplace.
- Be a role-model for WLB.

Discussion Questions

1. Do you know which of your employees are currently experiencing WLC?
2. Are you prepared to discuss WLC and WLB with your direct reports?
3. What policies and resources does your organization have in place to support employee WLB?
4. Do you have a healthy integration of you work life and your non-work life?

References

Braun, S., & Peus, C. (2018). Crossover of work–life balance perceptions: Does authentic leadership matter? *Journal of Business Ethics, 149*(4), 875–893. https://doi.org/10.1007/s10551-016-3078-x

Ernst Kossek, E., Kalliath, T., & Kalliath, P. (2012). Achieving employee wellbeing in a changing work environment. *International Journal of Manpower, 33*(7), 738753. https://doi.org/10.1108/01437721211268294

Fouché, C., & Martindale, K. (2011). Work–life balance: Practitioner well-being in the social work education curriculum. *Social Work Education, 30*(6), 675–685. https://doi.org/10.1080/02615479.2011.586566

Gravador, L., & Teng-Calleja, M. (2018). Work–life balance crafting behaviors: An empirical study. *Personnel Review, 47*(4), 786–804. https://doi.org/10.1108/PR-05-2016-0112

Griffiths, A., Harper, W., Desrosiers, P., Murphy, A., & Royse, D. (2019). "The stress is indescribable": Self-reported health implications from child welfare supervisors. *The Clinical Supervisor, 38*(2), 183–201. https://doi.org/10.1080/07325223.2019.1643433

Isaacs, D. (2012). For the love of labour. *Journal of Pediatrics and Child Health, 48*(11), 953–954. https://doi.org/10.1111/j.1440-1754.2012.02591.x

Jang, S., Zippay, A., & Jang, S. (2011). The juggling act: Managing work-life conflict and work-life balance. *Families in Society, 92*(1), 84–90. https://doi.org/10.1606/1044-3894.4061

Kalliath, P., & Kalliath, T. (2015). Work–family conflict and its impact on job satisfaction of social workers. *British Journal of Social Work, 45*(1), 241–259. https://doi.org/10.1093/bjsw/bct125

Kossek, E., & Lautsch, B. (2008). *CEO of me: Creating a life that works in the flexible job age.* Philadelphia, PA: Wharton School Publishing.

Lambert, E., Pasupuleti, S., Cluse-Tolar, T., Jennings, M., & Baker, D. (2006). The impact of work-family conflict on social work and human service worker job satisfaction and organizational commitment: An exploratory study. *Administration in Social Work, 30*(3), 55–74. https://doi.org/10.1300/J147v30n03_05

Rao, I. (2017). Work-life balance for sustainable human development: Cultural intelligence as enabler. *Journal of Human Behavior in the Social Environment, 27*(7), 706–713. https://doi.org/10.1080/10911359.2017.1327391

Sánchez-Vidal, M., Cegarra-Leiva, D., & Cegarra-Navarro, J. (2012). Gaps between managers' and employees' perceptions of work–life balance. *The International Journal of Human Resource Management, 23*(4), 645–661. https://doi.org/10.1080/09585192.2011.561219

Talukder, A., Vickers, M., & Khan, A. (2018). Supervisor support and work–life balance. *Personnel Review, 47*(3), 727–744. https://doi.org/10.1108/PR-12-2016-0314

Wu, L., Rusyidi, B., Claiborne, N., & McCarthy, M. (2013). Relationships between work–life balance and job-related factors among child welfare workers. *Children and Youth Services Review, 35*(9), 1447–1454. https://doi.org/10.1016/j.childyouth.2013.05.017

Index

Note: Page numbers in **bold** indicate a table on the corresponding page.

360-degree feedback 47, **49**

accountability 94–95
alliances: supervisory 6–7; therapeutic 6–7; working 5–11, 9
ambivalence 65–66, 69
Appreciative Inquiry (AI) 39, 74–75
asking questions **9**, **40**
assessment 44–51

Belbin's Team Roles **49**
biopsychosocial assessment 38
boundaries 111–118
Brief Strategic Therapy (BST) 22
burnout 122–123

case studies: and assessment 41–42; and boundaries 117–118; and evaluation 97–99; and intervention 60–61, 76–78; and observation 35; and onboarding 25–26; and resistance 67–69; and setting expectations 17–18; and staff development 88–89; and termination 105–107; and vicarious trauma 125–126; and work–life balance 133–134; and working alliances 9–11
change 63–69
client orientation 21–22
client termination 102–103
clinical interview 37–38
Cognitive Behavioral Therapy (CBT) 72
compassion fatigue 122–123
Competing Values Assessment **49**
crisis communication 59
crisis intervention 56–62
crisis management 55–62, **60**

diagnoses 38
Diagnostic and Statistical Manual of Mental Disorders (DSM) 32
DiSC Assessment **49**
documentation 32, 35
domestic violence 121
dual relationships 112–113

elephant and rider 66
empathy 40
employee orientation 20–26, **24**
employee retention 104
employee turnover 104
engagement 5–11
exit interviews 104
expectations 13–19, **17**

favoritism 115–117
Feedback Informed Treatment (FIT) 46
first 90 days 23
Focused Conversation Method 40–41, **40**

Gallup 12 questions (Q12) 15, 84
Gallup StrengthsQuest 87
goal setting 16–18
group dynamics 32–33

in-group relationships 7
Institute of Cultural Affairs 40–41, **40**
Interviewing 37–43, **40**
involuntary separation **105**

Leader Member Exchange (LMX) 6–7, 114
listening 31–32

Index 137

Management by Objectives (MBO) 74
Managing and Adapting Practice (MAP) 46
Maslach Burnout Inventory **49**
Maslow's hierarchy of needs 15, 84
metrics 46
Minnesota Multiphasic Personality
    Inventory (MMPI) 45, 47
motivation 7
Motivational Interviewing (MI) 65–69, **67**
Myers–Briggs Type Indicator **49**

National Association of Social Workers
    (NASW) 86, **88**
Network for Social Work Management
    (NSWM) 87
new employee orientation 22–26, **24**

observation 31–36, **34**
onboarding 20–26, **24**
organizational change 65–66
Organizational Culture (Schein) 32–33
organizational socialization 24
Outcome Rating Scale (ORS) 46
out-group relationships 7

Perceived Organizational Support (POS) 7–8
performance data 93–95
performance issues 71–78
performance monitoring 92–99, **97**
performance review 92–99, **97**
periodic review 92–99
personal development 84–86
Problem Solving Therapy (PST) 22, 72–75
professional development 86, **88**

rapport building 5, 23
reflective supervision 87
resistance to change 63–69, **67**
risk management 59
rituals 104
romantic relationships 113, 115
Routine Outcome Monitoring (ROM) 94

safety assessment 59–60
Secondary Traumatic Stress (STS)
    120–127, **124**
Self-actualization 84–85
self-care 120–127, 129–134
self-disclosure 113–115
Session Rating Scale (SRS) 46
setting expectations 13–19, **17**
sexual relationships 113, 115
SOAP notes 32
social media 59, 113–116, **116**
socializing 115–116, **116**
Solution Focused Brief Therapy (SFBT)
    72–75, **75**
solution focused management 74–75, **75**
solution focused supervision 74, **75**
staff development 81, 83–90, **88**
staff retention 23
staff turnover 23, 123
Stages of Team Development 47–48
Strengths-Based Management 74
stress 23, 40, 57, 77, 85, 86, **88**, **97**, 131
supervision 9, 95–99, **97**
supervision notes **9**
supervisory alliance 6–7

termination 101–107, **105**
Thematic Apperception Test (TAT) 45
therapeutic alliance 6–7
trauma 120–121
trauma-informed organizations 123–124
treatment monitoring 93–94

Vicarious Trauma (VT) 120–127, **124**
voluntary separation 105

Work–Life Balance (WLB) 129–134,
    132–133
Work–Life Conflict (WCT) 130, 134
workplace design 33

Z Process **49**